Principles
of
Creation

Principles
of
Creation

Manifesting Your Finest and Best

by

Anthony A. Bryce

Scripture quotations noted (KJV) are from the **King James Version** of the
bible. Used by permission, all rights reserved.

Scripture quotations noted (NIV) are from the **New International Version**
of the bible. Used by permission, all rights reserved.

Paperback ISBN 1 904908 26 8

Published by

Olive Publishing
The Olive Project
PO Box 1284
Huddersfield
West Yorkshire
HD5 8ZW

+ 44 (0) 1484 310856
info@olivefriends.com
www.olivefriends.com

Produced by Central Publishing Services of West Yorkshire

About Us

Anthony and Denise Bryce are the founders, directors and senior practitioners of *Olive Branch* – a Christian training provider whose purpose is to provide optimum living Christian education through inventive learning programmes and personal coaching. Through our Programmes we study, practice and teach biblical principles and practices of optimum Christian living and support believers towards increased personal effectiveness and well being in all areas of human life and activity. We deliver optimum living Christian education programmes to address issues of Leadership Education; Pastoral Care; Christian Living; Venture Education; Evangelism; Church Health; Biblical Theology and support Programme participants through one to one learner support via *Olive Friends*. Our work is supported by Associates who have been trained in the philosophy and delivery techniques of The Olive Project.

Independent of *Olive Branch*, Anthony & Denise Bryce are also the founders and directors of The **O**ptimum **L**iving **E**ducation Project – also known as *The Olive Project*. The Olive Project is a training and personal development consultancy whose purpose is to provide optimum living education and personal coaching by appealing to universal wisdom principles that are consistent with the Judeo-Christian Scriptures. Olive Programmes address issues of Personal Development; Youth Enrichment; Family and Parenting Support; Health Education; Social Regeneration and Life Long Learning in ways that stimulate learning, enjoyment and personal change.

Qualified in social work, adult education and training and mentoring, Anthony is an experienced family learning practitioner, trainer, PSHCE tutor and parenting support facilitator who has worked with children, young people and adults of all ages and backgrounds since 1989. Denise Bryce, his wife and partner in The Olive Project, is an advice and guidance practitioner, career coach and life skills trainer who has worked in public and private sector organisations with adults and youths since 1991.

About the Book

Principles of Creation - Manifesting Your Finest and Best, describes the processes and the significant learning experiences of the journey of my desire to bring my unique contribution into the earth. The Book speaks of the 'Joseph' journey of young man with grand thoughts and great enthusiasm and the typical frustrations, disappointments and challenges and the processes of personal growth and change inherent in such journeys. However, rather than being a biographical account of my life, the Book describes the processes of the journey, from desire to destiny, within a principle-centred framework.

Principles of Creation is essentially a study of the dynamic processes and principles involved in the biblical account of Creation and how these principles and processes can be practically applied to our own work of creation, personally and vocationally. In keeping with the aims of our work, the book has been written to inform, support and guide the ability inherent in each person to manifest their finest and best work. The Book began as a collection of ideas for our *Olive Personal Development Project: Tips from the Top*, and comes to you as an eight week action plan that will help you to design, develop and deliver in your own image, a worthy enterprise, quality of life, vision of your future.

Each day you will be introduced to an idea or concept, principle or strategy from the biblical account of Creation and will be given an assignment that will help you to practically apply the principles of creation to your life and life's work. On the Sabbath of each week you will be invited to review the themes of the week and to make decisions about how you intend to follow through. Principles of Creation will appeal to people who have a burning desire to turn their good ideas and grand thoughts into organised and intelligently directed plans of action, especially those who have known frustration with the fruits of their life and life's work. Principles of Creation includes a glossary of *Olive Concepts* and concludes with an outline of the *Olive Venture Coaching Plan.*

Foreword

I am confident that this book will go a long way towards your realising the potential of your Creator, in whose image you were created. You are, after all, His finest and best, a new species of being fashioned in the image of God to co-create with Him in the earth. I speak personally when I say that if you follow through on these principles they will work for you. My wife and I applied these 'Principles of Creation' to make significant changes in lifestyle and when setting up The Olive Project and have conducted *Olive Talks, Olive Resource Groups, Olive Seminars* and *Olive Projects* and provided *Olive Venture Coaching* to private individuals and small to medium enterprises (SMEs) based on the themes of the book. We have seen many people follow through on the ideas of this book with good results. *We desire the same for you and for others through you!*

By addressing you the reader in a personal way, as is my intention throughout this book, I wish to awaken the potential of your Creator within you. For, *"the greatest good you can do for another is not just to share your riches with him but to reveal to him his own."* (Benjamin Disraeli (1804 ~ 1881) I write especially to awaken those in Christ to their destiny and to encourage in them a desire and will to use all their powers to the glory of God and the outworking of His purposes in the earth.

Anthony A Bryce

Founder, director
& senior practitioner

Acknowledgements

I must first thank God my Creator and loving heavenly Father for the gift of life and for the many good people I have encountered on my 'Joseph' journey, none dearer to me than my wife Denise Bryce and my son Joseph. Denise has been on the journey with me since 1993 and has been a constant friend and companion throughout. Were it not for her encouragement and faith in the dreamer and in the dream, I would not have had the confidence to begin again. Thank you!

I must also give credit to my son Joseph, who whilst I was working on the book waited patiently for daddy to, "come off the computer and play." You are a joy and a blessing and a constant reminder to me of what is most important.

To my mum, Idaline, I owe so much. The prayerful support you provided, like only a mother can, has sustained me for such a time as this. For this I am eternally grateful.

I dedicate this book to my dad, the late Alexander Bryce. Thank you for a great start and 21 wonderful years. 'One son' salutes you!

Tony

A Bag of Tools

Isn't it strange that princes and kings,
and clowns that caper in sawdust rings,
and common people, like you and me,
are builders for eternity?

Each given a bag of tools
a shapeless mass, a book of rules.
And each must fashion, ere life is flown,
A stumbling block, or a stepping-stone.

---

first published 1941
Poems that Touch the Heart
compiled by A. L. Alexander

Contents

Week 1

Day 1. In His Image   13-15
The origins of your creative potential

Day 2. It Starts When You ……   16-18
Your ability to make things happen

Day 3. Conceiving Ideas   19-21
Generating good ideas

Day 4. The Seed Of An Idea   22-24
The potential in small things

Day 5. Burning Desire   25-27
The fire of desire that burns within

Day 6. Inside-Out   28-30
Releasing the fire of desire

Day 7. Sabbath Week 1:   31-33
A Summary of Week 1

Week 2

Day 8. What Do You Want?   37-39
The power of clarity

Day 9. Can You See It?   40-42
The power of visualisation

Day 10. Can You Describe It ?   43-45
Making your imagination work for you

Day 11. Why Do You Want It?   46-48
The power of self knowledge

Day 12.   How Comes After What And Why   49-51
The principle of corresponding action

Day 13. A Definite Decision To Begin   52-54
The power of a decision

Day 14.   Sabbath Week 2   55-56
A Summary of Week 2

Week 3

Day 15. Beginning   59-61
The principle of making a start

Day 16. First Things First   62-64
Beginning well

Day 17. Out Of Nothing   65-67
Faith to begin

Day 18. Beginning Again   68-70
The courage to start again

Day 19. What Have You Got?   71-73
Perceiving potential

Day 20. Utilising What You Have   74-76
Success is in your hands

Day 21.   Sabbath Week 3   77-78
A Summary of Week 3

Week 4

Day 22.   Let Us   81-83
Together we can

Day 23. Whose Us?   84-86
The characteristics of your let us team

Day 24. Talking Answers   87-89
Speaking the vocabulary of faith

Day 25. What Do You Think?   90-92
Drawing on the grace that resides in another

Day 26. We Accord   93-95
The power of agreement

Day 27. I Accord!   96-98
The principle of personal commitment

Day 28. Sabbath Week 4   98-101
A Summary of Week 4

Week 5

Day 29. From Head To Hand   105-107
From thinking to doing

Day 30. It Is Written   108-110
Your mission statement

Day 31. Planning Your Work   111-113
The 5WH approach

Day 32. SMART Goals   114-116
The principle of coherent delivery

Day 33. The Power In Doing   117-119
The miracle of activity

Day 34. Doing What You Do Best   120-122
Playing to your strengths

Day 35 Sabbath Week 5   123-124
A Summary of Week 5

Week 6

Day 36. Building By Design   127-129
    Working your plan

Day 37. Building On The Previous   130-132
    The power of momentum

Day 38. Formative Evaluations   133-135
    Mid course corrections

Day 39. In Your Image   136-139
    Inside-out

Day 40. Put Life Into It   140-142
    The power of personal investment

Day 41. Working The Laws Of Life   143-145
    Building by what works

Day 42. Sabbath Week 6   146-147
    A Summary of Week 6

Week 7

Day 43. Speaking Well   151-154
    The words that will work for you

Day 44. Delegation And Partnership   155-157
    People empowerment

Day 45. Core Values And Core Business   158-160
    Majoring on major things

Day 46. Growth Potential   161-163
    The abundance mentality

Day 47. Multiple Streams Of Supply   164-166
    Keeping yourself refreshed

Day 48. Threats From Within   167-170
   What lies beneath

Day 49. Sabbath Week 7   171-173
   A Summary of Week 7

Week 8

Day 50. Threats from Without   177-179
   The enemy at the door

Day 51. Seeing the Challenges Through   180-182
   The stamina of patience

Day 52. Summative Evaluations   183-185
   Seeing the end of your faith

Day 53. Celebrating Success   186-188
   Well done good and faithful servant

Day 54. The Big Picture   189-191
   Built to last!

Day 55. Continuing Without You   192-194
   Passing the baton on

Day 56. Sabbath Week 8   195-197
   A Summary of Week 5

Appendix

Olive Venture Coaching Plan   199-200

Olive Concepts   201-210

Olive Programmes   211-213

WEEK 1

Day 1 - In His Image

Everything within our time-space continuum is an effect that has been first caused by the activity of God and/or the activity of the works of His hand, principally the human being— both being capable of taking a thought, a desire, an idea, from their fertile imaginings to manifest the physical reality of that thought, desire, idea. But how is this possible for the human being? According to the Scriptures, the human being is the crown of God's creative involvement in the earth, the pinnacle of the works of His hand, a truly awesome species of being created in the Image of an Awesome God who imagined and created us deliberately and uniquely for Himself. *(Psalm 8:4; Revelation 4:11)* It is this distinguishing feature, being created in the image of an invisible God, which sets the human being apart from all other species of being.

In essence, the Creator animated the human being with His life giving Spirit and the human being became a co-creator with God in the earth, capable of acting on behalf of God. *(Genesis 2:7)* By creating us, *"in His image and likeness"*, *(Genesis 1:26)* with the addition of an awesome physical body, suited for life on planet earth, the Almighty Creator effectively appointed our kind, the human being, as His representatives on the earth. By virtue of our unique creation, the Almighty God, who is infinite in wisdom and awesome in power, also endowed our kind with great power— incredible potential for good, when submitted to the will of God. *(Genesis 11:6)* He gave us the power to speak, think, imagine, decide, choose, know, understand, learn, experience, grow, take action - to essentially become, ever increasingly who we are and what we are capable of, because of what He had imagined.

The Psalmist had in mind our unique creation when he remarked, *"we are fearfully and wonderfully made." (Psalm 139: 14KJV)* At the lowest level, having abilities as stated - our humanity, and at a higher level, our capacity to know, relate to and experience God.

Every individual possesses powers and resources of various sorts, by virtue of being a human being created in the image of an Awesome God. It is this unique distinction of our creation

13

that is the sole grounds for a healthy and right view of self. From such an elevated position we find our identity, understand our significance to God and fulfil our place alongside others in the universe. But what is a human being, really, and why does God care for us as He does? *(Psalm 8:4)* Why has He highly exalted the human being and why is His mind full of good thoughts about this particular species of being? *(Job 7:14)*

> Contrary to popular thought: *"You are not a bag of genes. You are not a bundle of conditioned reflexes. You are not a two-legged animal with an overgrown intellect. You are not your car, your job, your clothes, income, house, watch, or savings account. You are not a large blob of hormones. You are not a slave of brain chemicals. You are not a cluster of instincts. You are not a bucket of flaws. You are not a puppet of television, music, video games, pop culture, or peer pressure. You are not a self in desperate need of esteem. You are not the end product of events that happened when you were two. You are not measured by the size of your salary, expense account, or stock options."* *[www.livereal.com]*.

As a distinct and unique species of being, human beings possess the potential of **Elohim**; to create their own reality, each of us being capable of doing this for ourselves, whilst contributing something to the reality of others. Thus, the world we now know and live in is not entirely the world the Creator had in mind, it is, however, the world that we have created because of the choices we make and the laws we break. Our present reality is the product of our most dominant thoughts, words and deeds.

The more you understand and work with these biblical truths about your true self and your unique *nature/nurture experience,* the greater your scope for optimum living. Nothing about a person's potential is fixed or static— what and how much we make of ourselves and how we use our various and differing gifts, abilities, aptitudes, talents, skills, physical, mental, emotional and material resources, are spiritual issues that each person must act on with positive intent. Each one of us is more capable than we have realised. The Giver of **first and second birth potential** has given to each of us the joyous task of discovering, developing and maximising our potential for the greater good and has shown us, in the Scriptures, how to use our powers and resources for the greatest good. We do well to submit our powers and resources to biblical wisdom and truth so that what we make happen and bring into the earth honours God.

In your notebook, write down at least 20 statements beginning with 'I am.' These should be statements about your first and second birth potential! What do these statements reveal about who you are and what you are capable of?

First Birth Potential — Personal Power— Self Concept— Self-Esteem— Self Confidence— Human Givens Christian Education— Second Birth Potential — Nature/Nurture Experience

"Compared to what we ought to be, we are only half awake. We are making use of only a small part of our physical and mental resources. The human individual lives too far within his limits. He possesses power of various sorts which he habitually fails to use." William James (1842 ~ 1910)

Day 2 - It Starts When You...

The Bible opens with an incredible presupposition, an emphatic statement of faith, *"In the beginning God created the heavens and the earth" (Genesis 1:1).* According to the Scriptures the heavens and the earth, the whole universe, has its origins with a personal Being - ***Elohim.***

Elohim is represented throughout the Scriptures as the self-existent, self-conscious, self-determining, eternal Being of faith who brought into existence the universe as He had imagined it. It was Elohim who decided what the universe would consist of and determined the purpose it would serve in the grand scheme of things. It was Elohim, who by the power of His word commanded the universe to exist, and having commanded it to exist, orders it along its planned course, upholds and sustains it and directs all things to their appointed end. It all started with Him and would not have come into being if it were possible for Him to hold Himself back from being all that He is and is capable of within Himself. Had Elohim not ***deliberately*** exercised His potential as the Almighty God to act on what He was capable of, we would never know Him. The universe, being a general revelation of God, would never be a wonder to ponder if He had chosen not to release His creativity to create something outside of Himself. It would have remained hidden from view and unrealised.

As a unique species of being created in the image of Elohim, you are capable of much - a whole lot more than what has so far been realised. However, what you are capable of will benefit no one until ***you*** deliberately act on your *"I am"* statements. Self – knowledge and potential are never enough, they have to be released and exercised so that what is possible can become an actual physical reality for all to behold. As a purposeful being, you are required to take personal responsibility for designing, delivering and managing the reality that you imagine and create.

The more responsibility you take for the actions and outcomes of your life, the more your life will resemble the life you have in mind. If you wait for others to do things for you, they may not— you may also get what you do not want. Your life is too precious to leave to chance or in someone else's hands. Your life is not some natural process that will happen anyway, nor is it something that fate has determined, so that try as you might you cannot escape what is meant. The *locus of control* doesn't reside outside of you but within *you*. The power to decide and to follow through is yours to exercise. Not even the Almighty Creator will undermine your ability to chose and decide for yourself. Your life requires you to be its author, so that you write what is right and create your own unique story for the world to read.

So what could you do to plumb your inner depths, to release the potential yet to be realised, to uncover the powers that long to be recognised and developed? What could you read, learn, develop, arrange, invest in, do, work on, commit to, try your hand at or change? What do you presently know about what lies within you? What are you capable of?

There's no telling what you could do, achieve, know, accomplish, master, create, build, make happen for yourself and for others if you turned on all your powers and intelligently went after what you have been imagining. Frankly, there's no knowing and no telling until you do! There are depths in you that you have yet to discover, potential yet to be realised and powers crying out to be recognised and developed. This is not just true of you; it is true of every human being. What you have within you has to be drawn out. A demand has to be placed on it or the potential that you possess will not be seen. No one will know what you know if you do not make it known! Rather than wait for an external demand to put pressure on your potential, stir yourself up to become everything God has imagined for you. The change that you want to see in your personal world will be a reflection of the changes that will happen within you once you learn to turn on your own light.

The crux of personal responsibility centres on your desire and decision to take necessary and consistent actions upon your potential. This is a decision that is yours alone to make! The people you admire and esteem, the true achievers in life, did not wait for another person to get them started. They did not wait around for a break in their circumstances. Nor did they spend long hours gazing upon the achievements of another, wishing that they had more going for them. Instead they decided that things would be different because *they* could be different and took responsibility for making the changes themselves.

 In your notebook, write down your reply to this question. If you really went for it, what could you accomplish, achieve, know, master, create, build and make happen for yourself and for others?

 Locus of Control— Personal Responsibility— Personal Power— Self Efficacy Beliefs— Personal Empowerment

 "We all walk in the dark and each of us must learn to turn on our own light." Earl Nightingale

Week 1
Day 3 - Conceiving Ideas

 The universe owes its origins to Him who is without beginning— God. Everything about it reflects the wisdom, beauty, sovereignty, authority and glory of God. *(Romans 1:19-20)* It is truly an awesome wonder to ponder, a stupendous 'conception' of the eternal God– the physical manifestation of an idea He had in eternity past. But how did God come by such a big idea? Who instructed Him? From whom did He learn the art and science of creation? What laws of nature did He have to comply with? What authority did He consult and whose approval did He obtain? What previous work was His inspiration? Who determined what it would look like: its size and composition, the purpose it would serve and the time of its birth? God alone is responsible for it all! He imagined it and saw it before it existed and by the power of His word, commanded matter, energy and space to exist and to be continuously arranged according to His design. The big idea of the universe was conceived and nurtured by Him. He is its Author and the source of all origins within it. *"The true God, the mighty God, is the God of ideas."* *Alfred Victor Vigny. (1797-1863)*

 Although we are not sufficient within ourselves to create as God, we are capable of more than we have allowed ourselves to know. Like God, we are capable of taking a thought, a desire, an idea from our fertile imaginings to manifest the physical reality of that thought, desire or idea. But where do these ideas come from? How does a person conceive worthwhile ideas, thoughts, plans and schemes? Must they come to the recipient like a bolt of lightning? Is there any significance in an idea that you have developed yourself, over a period of time? Must it be something that no other person has previously considered? What do you think? To get to a handle on today's theme, let's begin where we began two days ago, the same place God began - knowledge of self.

The ideas you feel most passionate about and keen to invest in will be the ones that are consistent with who you are and the things that matter most to you. If you know yourself as well as you could, you will have a good idea about what you like, want, feel, desire, notice, dream of, and get angry about. As a result you will be predisposed towards imagining and creating things that matter to you and will be drawn towards opportunities that arouse and place a demand on your potential. *"Generally speaking, men are influenced by books which clarify their own thought, which express their own notions well, or which suggest to them ideas which their minds are already predisposed to accept."* *Carl Lotus Becker (1873-1945).* If you do not know yourself as well as you ought, I suggest you make every effort to get to know yourself better, for God has put within you and within your reach the resources that you require to bring your unique contribution into the world. If you do not know what He has placed within you, you will be unaware of the purpose that requires your being on the planet and ignorant of what your life has been about.

What better way to conceive ideas that benefit humanity and serve a purpose that transcends our temporal plane, than in the presence of God? In the secret place of prayer we connect with the Well Spring of Life and experience the immanence of His Presence. There in His Presence, ideas of eternal significance are conceived, take shape, receive divine impetus, and take on new meaning. As we still ourselves before Him, feed our minds with His Word and open up to Him in absolute trust, we make ourselves receptive to thoughts, ideas and actions that are divinely inspired.

The same is true of our worship of God. As we worship before our Creator our lives and our life's work take on new significance. There in His presence His thoughts, His priorities, His wishes become more important than our own— our visions are shaped by Him and come under His quiet influence. As we sit before the preached word of God with an opened mind, faith for action is aroused. *(Romans 10:17)* Similarly, by sharing heart with people of passion and purpose, especially around God's Word, ideas are conceived and further nurtured. Which is why devotional praying and corporate worship, preaching, teaching and Christian fellowship are important to your life and why it is important to be among people who have an avid interest in learning, change, growth and ideas. People who draw out what is in you and provoke you to growth.

Studies have shown that there is also tremendous value in thinking on paper. By thinking and representing our initial ideas laterally, using links, associations and connections that are unrestrained and solutions focused, we stimulate our brain to draw on imaginative, inventive and useful information from the recesses of our creative potential. The process of putting pen to paper also has an embedding effect. Furthermore, giving voice to those ideas makes thinking a *multi-sensory activity*.

The ideas that are worth their weight in gold are the ideas that you develop further through *meditation* and follow through. As you fellowship with the idea that you want to see realised you will see new combinations of old elements. None of this happens without you— your active participation is required, which is why you need to think about what you are thinking about and to nurture the ideas that won't leave you alone. So, how do you nurture ideas? You think about them, you talk about them, you write them down, you give voice to them, you give voice to them, you give them your time and attention, you listen to them, you picture them in your mind, you get excited about them and you act on them. By so doing you make the generation of ideas a multi-sensory activity. The more time you spend with the idea the more real it will become to you.

Write down in your notebook an idea that you have had in mind for at least 12 months. State it simply, in no more than 2 sentences. How did you come by the idea?

Lateral Thinking - Mind Mapping – Meditation - Brainstorming

"What is unsought will go undetected." Sophocles (BC 495 ~ 406)
"If you wish to find, you must search. Rarely does a good idea interrupt you." Jim Rohn

Week 1
Day 4 - The Seed of an Idea

Contrary to variant religious and philosophical thought, the universe did not exist materially in God. It did not emanate out from God and it is not the outward manifestation of God. That would make the universe infinite and only God can lay claim to the attributes of deity. He alone is eternal and unchanging — matter, energy and space, are not! The Scriptures teach that God is a substantial Being. He is all His own! He is not part of or within any other. His Being is immaterial, invisible and without composition or extension. He is a self-conscious, self-determining, Absolute Being. There is nothing belonging to matter in Him. He is over and above, outside and beyond and distinct from the material world and yet immanently involved with it.

According to the Scriptures the universe and all within it is a temporal act of God, a divine conception, determined by the collective counsel of the Godhead— the product of 'mental' activity within the Godhead in eternity past. The Bible teaches that God imagined it, saw it before it existed and by the power of His word, commanded matter, energy and space to exist and to be continuously arranged according to His design. The notion of 'matter, energy and space being continuously arranged', is entirely consistent with the Scriptures and is not borne out of un-biblical evolutionary thought. Genesis teaches that *God Is*, and that everything within the physical realm that He has created has the potential within itself to *become*, to multiply, expand, increase and produce *after its kind*. Not because of the eternity of matter, but because of the awesome power and life that is in His Word. Every human being on the planet, every atom in a structure, every seed in the earth has the potential of Elohim residing within it.

The thoughts and ideas you conceive are like seeds, they have various yields of greatness within them, nurture them and they will share their greatness with you. Though they may not look anything like the fruit you anticipate they will bring forth at first, they have the inherent potential to abundantly yield of that fruit. Not by themselves, but because of the power and life that is in you to make those ideas reveal their potential. Though small and seemingly insignificant in appearance, when compared to what you are hoping for, they have the power to produce after their kind. The degree to which your ideas release their potential is largely down to you, the environment they grow up around, the condition of the soil in which they are planted in and the care and attention they are shown.

There's no telling what measure of harvest could come from a mustard seed of an idea that is planted in good ground, refreshed from above and attended to by diligent hands. Even the most miniscule of seeds can become more, when handled diligently. Thus, not only do you have creative potential within you (Day 1) the ideas that you conceive (Day 3) have potential with them (Day 4). As a co-creator in the earth, you must take personal responsibility for releasing your potential and the potential in your ideas. (Day 2) For **"human beings have the power to transform thoughts into physical reality; human beings can dream and make dreams come true."** *(Napoleon Hill)* So how is this done? How does a person transform large thoughts, into physical reality, from small beginnings?

 I know of no better way to arouse the potential within a seed than *faith* in the seed's ability to become more and a clear and compelling *vision* of what more might look like. Nothing stirs up the potential of a thing like a vision of that thing fully grown, revealed in all its glory.

For your ideas to become their full potential there must be a similar faith in you, an ambitious faith that will not be satisfied until the vision is fully realised. Like a seed, your ideas know what they are capable of and what they can grow into. They are not content to be a grain of potential, to just *be*, they want to *become* what was intended. This is why there is so much activity within a seed that is planted in good ground. It sees its opportunity to become more and draws its strength from the ground it is planted in and the environment that surrounds it.

For your seedling idea to yield its fruit, care must also be given to the environment that surrounds it and the state of the soil that feeds it. Impoverished, harsh, cold, staid external surroundings are not conducive to the growth of an idea. These environments stifle potential, choke creativity, resist change, ridicule ambition, frustrate progress and envy achievement. They do not know how and show little interest in discovering, developing and releasing potential. In these circumstances the seed has a greater struggle outwards and upwards. Ideas, like seed, need warmth, light, space and a commensurate degree of challenge to germinate and take root. This is their optimum environment.

Unlike the external environment that feeds your ideas from without, the soil feeds it from beneath; it is the most immediate environment of the seed. I am referring to the thoughts, beliefs, attitudes, self-talk, and behaviours that feed your ideas. The things that come out from you that either nurture or stifle your idea. Studies confirm that what you and I say, believe and do and the way we say, believe and do them has everything to do with the yield of our harvest of ideas. The greatest power to influence your big idea is within you. The more potential you unlock within yourself the more your ideas are nurtured. This is why what you are becoming will be your idea's best fruit and will produce the harvest of your life.

In your notebook, write down what the idea you identified yesterday could become if you went to work. What does the idea look like now?

Imagination – Aspiration – Ambition – Vision - Personal Development

"A mind stretched by a new idea never returns to it original dimensions." Oliver Wendel Holmes.

Week 1
Day 5 - A Burning Desire: The Spirit of Faith

The word 'enthusiasm' comes from Greek and means *God within (entheos).* It refers to a divine spark or fire that burns within the breast. The word describes well the activity within a seed and speaks of what was going on in the 'heart' of God when He conceived and nurtured the idea of the universe. According to the Scriptures, God is the *Living God,* who out of the abundance of His perpetually Being is continuously and perpetually creating, speaking, showing, doing, revealing and communicating Himself. He is described as Light and Life, a constant flow of creative potential.

It was out of the gross wealth of His thoughts that He brought into existence all things— the universe for His pleasure and the earth for our enjoyment. *(Revelation 4:11; Genesis 1:28)* Nothing that He creates is ever casual, by accident or incidental. Everything that He creates has involved investment of emotion and will on the part of God. The Scriptures teach that He determines their purpose, has a fatherly concern for the things He brings into existence and shows His loving kindness to the inhabitants of the earth, especially the human being. *(Matthew 5:45; Act 14:17)*

As a product of mental activity within the Godhead, the universe was something that burned, conceptually, within God before He spoke about it. It was a burning desire that came out of the overflow of His Person. According to the Scriptures, God the Father, Son and Holy Spirit met together in counsel, in eternity past, to determine and establish what would come to pass, before anything other than them existed. This was more than an intellectual exercise — positive emotions like 'delight' and 'pleasure' featured in their deliberations to create. The Scriptures teach that God spoke to Himself about what He had in mind before it came to be, - *"let us make man"* - *(Genesis 1:26)* and saw, felt, touched, tasted and handled through *meditation* the idea of the universe before it existed. *(Ephesians 1:11-12)* Then, out of the abundance of His heart, spoke, commanding it to be as He had imagined.

 If an idea is the product of mental activity, whereby the mind consciously conceives and nurtures a thought, *enthusiasm* is the emotional and volitional aspects of an idea: *"the irresistible surge of will and energy to execute your ideas."* (Henry Ford) Enthusiasm, by definition, is a desire that has not only captured the imagination; it is sparked and fuelled by it. It has been described as the starting point of all achievement, for it gives life and energy to our thoughts and ideas. It takes them off the page and out of our heads and provides the stimulus required to make them real. By burning desire I am referring to a definite and consuming passion, a healthy obsession, the driving force that informs decisions, stimulates action and propels people towards their life purpose and vision. I call this burning desire a healthy obsession because it is not a fire of dangerous passions that rages without internal control or management, but a directed energy force that knows how to ebb and flow effectively towards the object of its desire. There is no risk of burn out with such a healthy obsession because the person who has a healthy obsession has learned the important lessons of self- regulation - how to work, rest and play proportionately.

A burning desire is one of the key characteristics of the innovators, originators, and creators of our world, people who, having *learned to switch on their light*, get excited about the potential that resides within them and the positive possibilities that can be produced. These people have strong *self-efficacy beliefs,* take *personal responsibility* for how their life and work turns out and are highly motivated *from within.* They willingly and enthusiastically take necessary and consistent steps towards the impression that they want to make real. This is why when threatened by severe opposition and extremely challenging circumstances they have enough resolve, determination and faith within them to carry them through. They possess an internal fire that will not be quenched from without.

Burning desires are fuelled by *ambition* and *imagination*— the pull from without and within, caused by a large vision of the future. Such a vision is created by thinking bigger than the present situation. The more you meditate on an idea that you have conceived, even though it can be compared to a 'grain of mustard seed', the more that idea will grow in you.

The ideas that you nurture **will** affect you. They will engender within you the enthusiasm of faith, causing you to believe that all things are possible and that the idea can be made a physical reality. For ideas to affect you like this you have to fellowship with them, meaning, you have to see, feel, touch, taste and handle them through **meditation.**

Your best ideas will come out of the overflow of what burns within you, because of what you think about, listen and attend to, speak about, do habitually and have enthusiasm for. If you have not yet discovered for yourself the power of a burning desire, spend some time thinking about what interests and excites you. Think about what gets your attention, disturbs your sleep, gets you all fired up and eager to do something decisive? What motivates you to get up early, go the extra mile, work late, study, change, learn and grow? What is the great love of your life that will not let you go? What has left you with a hunger so deep that it must be satisfied? What cries out deep within you and refuses to be silenced? If you had difficulty with these questions, ask someone to help you draw out what is in you and to **coach** you through to understanding.

What emotional effect does the idea from day 3 have on you?
What feelings and thoughts does it arouse within you?

Passion – Desire - Enthusiasm

"The ideal life is in our blood and never will be still. Sad will be the day for any man when he becomes contented with the thoughts he is thinking and the deeds he is doing - where there is not forever beating at the doors of his soul some great desire to do something larger, which he knows that he was meant and made to do." Phillips Brooks (1835-93)

Week 1
Day 6 - Inside-Out: The Principle of Faith

 God spoke to Himself about what He had in mind before He acted; saw, felt, touched, tasted and handled through *meditation* the idea of the universe before it existed and then, *out* of the abundance of His heart, spoke, commanding it to be as He had imagined. Because God is the Living God, He is continuously and perpetually *speaking, showing, creating, doing, communicating* and *revealing* something of Himself in the earth. From what we know of His works we must conclude that He cannot be contained. He is boundless and transcends all spatial limitations of the universe. There is no place within or outside of the universe where He is not. He is measureless, unconfined and unlimited. It is impossible for Him to cease from being all that He is as God.

In addition to being the Living God, God is also the Sovereign Lord of the universe in that He acts deliberately and intelligently with authority. The Scriptures teach that God works His sovereign will in His entire creation, both natural and spiritual, according to His predetermined plan. A plan based on the foreknowledge, wisdom and goodness of God and the collective counsel of the Godhead. According to the Scriptures He makes happen whatever He has eternally decreed, by the power and activity of His Word. Thus, when God spoke His first recorded words, *"Light, Be!" (Genesis 1:3)* He was beginning to call into existence what He had been thinking about. When used in this context, the principle of inside-out refers to spoken words and actions of faith that express, confirm, reveal and empower our ideas, desires, intentions, wishes and thoughts. In relation to God, it refers to His ability to manifest what He has decreed, simply by giving voice to it.

 Everything around you did not just come to be, but came out of an idea or thought that someone had *and* did something about because they thought it possible and desirable to externally

28

manifest what they had conceived as an idea. Much of what you see around you confirms that the ideas that you nurture and feel passionate about will provoke you to action. They will arouse within you the enthusiasm of faith, causing you to believe that all things are possible where there is *"an irresistible surge of will and energy to execute your ideas."* *(Henry Ford)*

For ideas to provoke you to action, as we saw on Days 3 & 4, you have to see, feel, touch, taste and handle them through **meditation** until out of the abundance of your heart you speak out and act on what is in you. The burning desire that we spoke of on Day 5 is not something that is easily quelled— creativity demands expression— what is going on within has to be released and intelligently directed.

The first place to locate passion and enthusiasm of this kind is in the words and language of those who have been affected by a compelling **vision.** Such people use colourful and inspiring words and language: to clarify thinking, to create mental pictures and images of the idea in full colour, to embed and develop their ideas, to provide food for thought, to give shape and structure to their ideas, to arouse their potential, to create light for understanding and greater awareness of what must be done to move the idea outwards, into the physical realm.

As well as being vehicles to clarify, express, describe and convey our grand ideas, intentions, wishes and thoughts, words also have an amazing ability to personally affect us, arousing either faith or doubt. Much of this type of verbal activity is internal self-talk, evidence that we have been thinking, feeling, seeing, hearing and nurturing ideas from within. Self-talk is extremely useful. *"Some of the most important conversations you hold in life are the ones you hold with yourself."* As the idea takes shape within us, because of positive self-talk, we find greater degrees of clarity, confidence and conviction to speak out what we have been thinking, feeling, seeing, hearing and nurturing. However, it is not just what we say that has creative potential, the strength of emotion and physical energy we invest in our words carry the greatest influence. Still, for all our confident speaking there is a danger, and it is this, that *"we have too many high-sounding words, and too few actions that correspond with them."* *(Abigail Adams, 1744-1818)* Or as Whitehead put it, *"Ideas won't keep; something must be done about them."* *(Alfred North Whitehead (1861-1947)*

By themselves, grand thoughts and confident language do not inherently possess the power to unlock the potential within our ideas—*corresponding activity* is required. By corresponding activity I am referring to purposeful actions that are consistent with our great ideas and words of faith. These actions correspond with, develop and take further our thoughts and ideas and take us towards manifesting the inner image that we have in mind. It is in the saying *and* in the doing that grand thoughts become tangible, perceptible physical realities.

If ideas remain in the head, they will produce nothing more than deluded individuals. People who think they are doing well because they have conceived a great idea. If ideas do not get beyond "high-sounding words", what we have are people with a lot to say but little to show for what they know. Where there is no commensurate, *self- expression* a person with a burning desire, unexpressed, will be incredibly frustrated. This happens because the burning desire gets turned inwards and becomes an unhealthy obsession that consumes away the individual. To progress our ideas and to keep our inner lives healthy and fertile we must take action. *Faith without corresponding action manifests nothing. (James 2:17)* What we have within us has to be released and intelligently directed outwards.

What immediate actions could you carry out to move the idea of day 3 forward?

Aspiration– Faith — Ambition - Frustration—Self Expression—Corresponding Activity-

"Action springs not from thought, but from a readiness for responsibility." Dietrich Bonhoeffer (1906-45)

Day 7
Sabbath Week 1

Before I invite you to make your personal confessions of faith and to decide on this weeks' corresponding action, I want to summarise for you what we have discovered to date and how we might put them to work.

 God is the unique, personal, self conscious, eternal being of faith, the almighty Creator of the universe and of planet earth. It was God who brought forth the whole visible and invisible universe without the use of pre-existent material, and gave it an existence, distinct from His own and yet always dependent on Him.

- God is the One who, by the power of His word, commanded the universe to exist and having commanded it to exist, orders it along its planned course upholds and sustains it and directs all things to their appointed end. It all originated and started with Him and would not have come into being if it were possible for Him to hold Himself back from being all that He is and is capable of within Himself. (Day 2) He chose to act!

- God is the Living God, who out of the abundance of His perpetually Being is continuously and perpetually creating, speaking, showing, doing, revealing and communicating, He is a constant flow of awesome creative potential. (Day 5) Because of Him the universe is an awesome wonder to ponder, a stupendous 'conception', the product of 'mental' activity within the Godhead in eternity past— the material substance of an idea that was in God, not materially or physically, but conceptually. (Day 4)

- As the Lord of the universe, God works His sovereign will in His entire creation, both natural and spiritual, through the awesome power and activity that resides within the words that He spoke over

31

the entire cosmos, in eternity past. It was this Word made flesh that manifested externally and supremely what was in God conceptually. (Day 6)

The human being is a unique species of being, created in the Image of an Awesome God, who imagined us and created us deliberately for Himself. The human being possesses incredible powers and potential because of what God has invested in us and destined for us. We are co-creators in the earth, ordained by God to be fruitful in every way imaginable, to make a mark on our environment and to exercise godly authority in and over the earth, as God does in Heaven.

- Everything within our time-space continuum is an effect that has been caused, either by the direct activity of God or the activity of the works of His hand, the human being. Like God we are capable of taking a thought, a desire, an idea, from our fertile imaginings to conceive and manifest the physical reality of that thought, desire, idea. Like God we must take personal responsibility for the release and use of our powers and potential and for the worlds we create with our imagination, words and actions. We must get to know who we are and what we are capable of and to give expression to all that we have within us and within our world.

- Not only do we have creative potential within us, the ideas that we conceive have growth potential with them. Like God we are capable of giving life to the ideas that we conceive and nurture.

- We nurture our thoughts and ideas by seeing, feeling, touching, tasting and handling them through meditation until out of the abundance of our heart, we speak out and support with corresponding actions the ideas and thoughts we wish to bring into the physical world.

I am a unique species of being, created in the Image of an Awesome God, who imagined me and created me deliberately for Himself. I possess incredible powers and potential because

of what God has invested in me and destined for me. I am a co-creator in the earth, ordained by God to be fruitful in every way imaginable, to make a mark on my environment and to exercise godly authority in and over the earth, as God does in Heaven. Like God I am capable of taking a thought, a desire, an idea, from my fertile imaginings to conceive and create my own physical reality. Like God I take personal responsibility for the release and use of my powers and potential and for the worlds I create with my imagination, words and actions. I make every effort to get to know who I am and what I am capable of and I chose each day to give expression to that which I have within me and to use the resources that reside within my world.

I accept that I not only have creative potential within me, the ideas that I conceive have growth potential with them. As a co-creator in the earth, I take personal responsibility for releasing my potential and for unlocking the potential in my ideas. I believe that my ideas will become more as I become more. I make every effort to learn, change and grow as a person. Like God I am capable of giving life to the ideas that I conceive and nurture. I decide today to see, feel, touch, taste, handle through daily meditation the ideas that I conceive, so that out of the abundance of my heart, I too can speak out of an overflow, commanding it to be as I have imagined. Not only will I speak out the ideas and thoughts that I wish to bring into the physical world, I will support them with corresponding actions.

Knowing what you know, what have you decided to do? What immediate action could you take that would move you towards the vision you have for your life and life's work? Who could you speak to? What new skills could you learn? What new disciplines could you develop? What further knowledge could you acquire? What attitudes and beliefs could you change? What plans could you rearrange? What new goals could you set? Whatever you decide to do, the ability to decide and to follow through resides with you! Your Success is in Your Hands!

WEEK 2

Week 2
Day 8 - What Do You Want?

 God already knew His heart and mind concerning our planet before He brought forth the heavens and the earth. The Scriptures teach that the Godhead had met in eternity past to determine and establish what would come to pass before anything other than them existed. As a result of their deliberations, God had a clearly defined purpose and a desired outcome in mind, an outcome that would be consistent with His ability and with what matters most to Him (His values).

Because God is a self-determining, purposeful being and knew what He wanted, He was able to intelligently direct His energies to bring into being what He had imagined. What God ultimately wanted came into being on day 6; everything prior to the creation of the human being was created in anticipation of our creation. What God wanted more than anything else, the thing that would give Him the most pleasure, would be to bring into existence a species of being made in His image that would love, worship, serve and lavishly enjoy Him in the earth. This is what He wants and has always wanted for the human being. It is His greatest affection, conceived before the foundation of the world, and He has never lost sight of it. It is the burning desire (Day 5) that moved Him to send His Son into the world— so that the will of God could be done in the earth as it's is being done in Heaven.

As the executive of God's vision for humanity, Jesus had intimate knowledge of the Father's vision, shared the same values and was willing to do what was necessary to make the will of God a reality in the earth. Consequently, He was not distracted from His purpose because He knew what He was about. He knew what He wanted His life to accomplish and sowed His life like a corn of wheat in the service of God, believing that He would see the fruits of His labour, the travail of His soul and be satisfied.

 Like a farmer who plants and nurtures a seed expecting the seed to produce fruit, the ideas that you have and the potential within you has a purpose, they are meant to produce after their kind. My question to you is what exactly? What do you want to be the outcome of your efforts? What are you hoping for and expecting to see? What will be the results of your life and the labour of your life? These are good questions to ask and to answer, because when you and I want something, we do certain *things*. There is always a reason why you do what you do. For example, why get up early, read, learn, study, refrain from certain attitudes and behaviours, change and work hardest on yourself? Because these actions are corresponding actions, necessary actions that will bring you towards the good life that you have imagined for yourself. So, what do you want, really?

Many people know what they *do not* want, and try their very best to steer clear of these things. What they find more difficult to conceive is a clear vision of what they *do* want. This question, for many, is more difficult to define and as a result many spend their lives being indifferent about the things that matter most and enthusiastic about the things that matter least. To come to a clear understanding of what you want, the place to begin is within. Ask yourself, what do I want more than anything else in the world? What really matters to me? Identifying what you truly want is something that you should take time over, understand and define for yourself.

It is not something that you let other people define for you; they just do not know you well enough and might just get you to invest time, effort and energy into something that is not what you want. There is no value in going after something outside of you that does not reflect your values. If what others want for you conflicts with who you are, you will not know personal fulfilment.

Another reason why it has to come out of you is because the vision—the external reality of what you are seeing — is more effectively realised when it reflects the inner image that you have of the thing. This will be an image that you have shaped according to your values, beliefs, abilities, priorities and affections, rather than an image imposed from without, that has been shaped by someone else. Knowing what you want and do not want will also help you to define your *success criteria—* how you will define and measure a successful outcome.

Once you are clear about what you want, make its realisation dependent on you becoming more, and make it sufficiently far reaching so that you keep learning, changing and growing in the direction of what you want. What ought to matter most to you is what you are becoming in pursuit of what you are wanting. Your personal development is far more valuable to you and to your world than any thing, because the yield of your harvest of ideas will be commensurate with your personal growth. More than anything external, studies show that people want to experience personal pleasure. It is often this desire to experience personal pleasure and fulfilment that is behind their pursuit of all things material. Those who tend to experience personal pleasure and fulfilment on a consistent basis have come to realise that there is no greater pleasure than experiencing in spirit, soul and body the incredible feelings that come with realising and fulfilling one's potential and life's purpose and the joy of being able to share who you are and what you are becoming with others.

In your notebook, write down what you expect the idea of last week to do for you. What does this say about what you truly want?

Goal Clarification—Success Criteria

"Decide what you want, decide what you are willing to exchange for it. Establish your priorities and go to work." H. L. *Hungt*

Week 2

Day 9 - Can You See It?

 Before God created the heavens and the earth He not only had a clear understanding of what He wanted, He also had a clear *vision* of what He saw, within Himself, and wanted to see, outside of Himself. Genesis tells us that at each juncture of creation, '*God saw and said that it was good*' *(Genesis 1:4, 10, 12, 18, 21, 25)* and that when He had concluded His work on the sixth day He saw it all and said that it was '*very good*'. (*Genesis 1:31*) The reason why He was able to say that it was '*good*' and '*very good*' is because what He was actually seeing, looked everything like what He saw, it looked like the inner image, the blue print of what He was expecting to see come into being.

Being omniscient, God not only saw the beginnings of planet earth; He also saw its end and everything in between, in one eternal and simple act. He saw its original beauty, the ravishing effects of the fall of humanity on His original design and His work of grace and restoration, which concludes with the heavens and the earth renewed. In one simple and eternal act, He was able to *see* it as He intended it to *look*, before it could be *seen,* was able to *see* the difference when it no longer *looked* like what He had in mind and was able to *see* what it would again *look* like when made new *(Revelation 21: 1—22:5)*. It was this completed vision of restored humanity that was His primary motivation, the eagerly awaited desired outcome that continues to receive His attention and concentration. It was for this very reason that the Son of God came into the earth— to fulfil God's vision of the future.

 It is good to know what you want and to be able to state it specifically and simply (Day 8). The more you hear it said and give credible and confident voice to it, the more you internalise it. However, to embed and experience what you are hearing and saying to yourself more deeply, you need to create a compelling vision of the completed picture. Visualising what you want is a powerful mental tool, for it moves you towards what you want becoming 'externalised.' By using your *imagination* to get a crisp, photographic image of what you want, you are mentally and emotionally designing in advance a compelling vision of the future. Such a vision of your life and life's work provides incredible motivation towards making it real.

So what is a vision? A vision is the picture in your mind that you see of what things will look like when all your goals have been achieved. It is an incredibly powerful visual tool because a compelling vision of the future will instil in you the passion to act, the courage to act, the motivation to act and the commitment to see the challenges through. A compelling vision of the future will help you focus on what to do next and what choices to make in a given situation. Without an appealing vision of the future and the means to make it possible, people drift and waste their energies on things that are not important. Where there is no vision, hope fades, motivation diminishes and courage flags. Possessing a vision can be likened to having an aim or a goal - an object towards which your earnest endeavours and resources can be directed. No forward steps are taken until a vision is established clearly in the mind and there is sufficient desire in the heart of the 'seer' to move towards it.

Because goals are important to the quality of one's life, to achievement and success, it is important that you know what they look like and how you create a compelling one. Here's how! 1. Get clear about what you really want (Day 8) and create a visual image of it in your mind. For each area of your life ask yourself, *"what do I want as a desired outcome in the following areas of my life: relationship to God, family, work, vocation, social life, personal finance, career, vacation, future, physical health, contribution in the world."* 2. Make sure that the image of what you want is consistent with your values, so that you know for sure that this is the goal for you. This will ensure that there is no conflict within you and that you are able to commit to it unreservedly (Day 11).

3. Make the picture or image compelling and attractive so that it pulls on your potential to learn and to grow as a person (Day 2). 4. Describe what you see using vivid, bright, colourful pictures, expressive language and gestures and

talk about what you see to yourself! If necessary, use words and a literary style like poetry, rhythm and rhyme, to make the picture affect you on a multi-sensory level. Add music: sing it, recite it, put it on tape and listen to it often, this will help embed the vision more fully (Day 43). 5. Write the vision down so you have a written record of it (Day 30). 6. Get excited about it, give it your attention and make it a priority (Day 5). 7. Working backwards from what you want and have visualised, ask yourself what needs to happen for the image to be created? 8. Break the vision down into measurable mini goals, objectives, so that they become small steps towards your large vision (Day 32). 9. Regularly revisit your mini goals and the big picture in order to keep yourself on track (Day 36). If you get off track, modify and change your approach towards your goals. 10. Put a date on each of your goals. Include timescales that allow for an objective to be immediately acted on and achieved within 24 hours, within a week, a month, within 2 years, 5 years 10 years, 20 years. Do this for each area of your life (Day 32).

11. When you are ready, go public with them (Day 16). Share your enthusiasm with a few like-minded people (Day 22) and don't be deterred by anyone or anything (Day 51). 12. Make their achievement dependent on *you* taking consistent actions towards them (Day 2). 13. Make them measurable, so that you receive constant feedback about how you are progressing. 14. When the big picture has been realised, enjoy the fruits of your harvest and share them with the people who have had a hand in bringing your ideas to fruition (Day 53).

In your notebook, write an opening paragraph of what you have envisioned will be the outcome of your life and life's work.

Visualisation

"Dream lofty dreams, and as you dream, so you shall become. Your vision is the promise of what you shall one day be; your ideal is the prophecy of what you shall at last unveil." James Lane Allen (1849-1923)

Week 2
Day 10 - Can You Describe It?

In Genesis chapter 1, God can be heard simply stating the outline of His unfolding vision for planet earth. What cannot be heard is a detailed description of what each thing will look like in their various varieties, shapes, sizes, colours and textures. On the basis of the skeletal outline of His public statements, God fleshed out His design for each living thing according to their genetic structure, and His plan and purpose for the human being in the earth according to His eternal decrees or blueprint. Because God is the Originator, Designer and Creator of the earth He knows everything there is to know about the genesis of the earth— how it was fashioned and every thing within it. He is able to describe it all in fine details. He knows because He was there in the beginning and has been present throughout. Not as an onlooker beholding a work of art that their hands did not fashion, but as the originator and creator of that work.

In chapters 38 and 39 of the book of Job we have recorded a conversation between God and Job about the specific details of Creation. The account makes it clear that God was personally involved in fashioning the details of His vision of planet earth. The account reveals God's detailed knowledge of the earth and Job's ignorance of God as the Designer and Creator of the universe. As Job is not the Creator of the heavens and the earth He does not have the answers to the questions put to him by God. God was essentially saying to Job in this descriptive account, *"as an onlooker you see the earth as it is and you enjoy it like a child with a gift, but I know the earth in the minutes of details for I am its author and parent. I brought it forth, I gave it life, I nurtured it and fashioned it and saw it through its various stages of development. I know things about it that no person can know for I was there in the beginning."* In addition to being the sovereign Lord, the Creator of heaven and earth, who commanded things to be, God is also involved with His vision on the 'ground', especially through the Word made flesh.

Having a vision is good, for vision creates a broad outline of what you have in mind and provides you with sufficient clarity to move you towards it. However, being able to vividly describe the vision goes much further in firing imagination, enthusiasm and action. Using your imagination to flesh out the details of your vision allows you to magnify the picture many times over so that the details are crisp. This is best done on paper, whilst in meditation or in silence, so that by writing freely you enable yourself to describe the vision in a multi-sensory way. Through your imagination you are able to describe what you can see, hear, touch, taste and smell, the moods, colours and the surroundings. By doing this you allow yourself to experience in advance the vision in full bloom. You get to see yourself in it, what you are doing, what you are wearing, who else is there, what they are doing, what can be heard, how you are feeling, what's going through you mind and a clear sense of how many, what size and how much. This information should be documented and retained (Day 30). Describing your vision to yourself in this way is extremely useful as the more you can bring the vision up close and personal the more realisable it will appear to you. Because a vision is the picture of what *you* want, it is up to you to fill in the details and to personalise it, to make it more meaningful to you and to put your unique mark on it

As you use your imagination to flesh out your vision it is important to understand that the small details of your vision is an entirely private matter, and not necessarily for public airing. What is important is that you say enough, as God did in Genesis 1, rather than everything. (Some things are for you alone, to hold in you heart until the physical reality catches up with your mental picture). It is also worth noting that the details that you produce when fleshing out your imaginings are not meant to serve as a checklist to ensure that every detail of your vision is carried out. As human beings we see in part and speak as we see, however, as we mature and get nearer to what we want, we see more clearly and care more about the essentials. Everything else is peripheral and subject to revision and further refinement.

The ability to describe your vision vividly is also important because it moves you, necessarily, towards thinking about— how? Because you are the designer and creator of your vision, you need to be involved in the details of the vision as it takes shape and is being realised. Thinking about the nuts and bolts of the vision shows that you appreciate that the big vision, the lofty ideal, the grand desire, the incredible idea, has to be owned and worked on by you. If your vision is going to be worthwhile and of value to God and humanity it cannot be something that someone else has worked on and presented to you completed and fully furnished. Rather, it has to be something that you have fashioned with your imagination and with your hands, (Day 40). This is important. If you have toiled and personally invested to see it realised, you will not let anyone or anything take it from you or talk you out of it (Day 51). You will be careful to look after what you have birthed. If your vision is going to look anything like how you imagined it, you will also have to design and create it as you see it. Your creative potential will not be fully satisfied until you design and fashion your vision in your own likeness and according to the inner image that you have of it (Day 39).

Building on yesterday's opening paragraph, flesh out what you have simply stated. Fill in the details, personalise it, make it more meaningful to you and put your unique mark on it.

Imagination

"Imagination is the voice of daring. If there is anything Godlike about God, it is that He dared to imagine everything." Henry Miller (1891-1980)

Week 2
Day 11 - Why Do You Want It?

 More than anything else in the world God wanted to bring into existence a species of being made in His image that would love, worship, serve and lavishly enjoy Him in the earth. Just ask yourself, what would a self-sufficient, self-determining, self-existent eternal Sprit want with a human being? Why create a species of being unlike any other and yet similar to the divine being? Was it because God had nothing else to do and thought He would test His creative potential? Was it because He was lonely and longed for company? Was it because He was in need of love and worship, praise and recognition? According to the Scriptures, none of these apply. God did not create the human being to meet a need within Him, nor did He create the human being because He was internally driven to do something unique outside of Himself. On the contrary, the Scriptures teach that God created this new species of being, the human being, so that He might share with the human being the wealth and richness of His eternal Being.

But why would He want to do this? Why would He endow the human being with the capacity to know, relate to and experience Him in all His goodness? Why take the risk of endowing the human being with the power to choose and to decide what they will set their affections upon? Surely it would have been better for God to retain His distinctiveness by being aloft and distant from us? According to the Word of God, God does what He does because that's **Who He Is!** He does what He does because He is love! God's why, His fundamental why towards humanity, is about His goodness and His selfless love for what He has created. His great motivation, His reason, His purpose, His desire, His holy passion is to deal bountifully and kindly with all His creatures and to give of Himself to us for our enjoyment and benefit. God's what and why are therefore consistent with and emerge out of His unchangeable character and divine nature.

Why is an important question that we have only ___ ___ considered because of its close relationship to what? It is an important question because, unlike 'what' which tends to be focused on an external object, why is fundamentally about matters of the heart— values, beliefs, motives, reasons, purpose and desires. Why is about what matter most to you! It is an important question because if you do not have a good enough why, a personal why, a compelling why, a why that is bigger than your personal goals and needs, a why that has the well being of others and the honour of God at its centre, what you are reaching for will not energise, sustain and satisfy your personal potential. As a result, you will lack the staying power to see the inevitable challenges through. A good why provides internal sustenance and energy, defines our boundaries, provides surefootedness and certainty, conviction, clarity and confidence.

A good enough why will focus you and will involve you in activities that will bring your unique contribution into the world. A good why will cause you to freely give of yourself. Some of the most common whys that people have based their life and life's work on include: *(Because I can. Because I want to! Because they want me to! Because I am good at it! What else is there? Because it's good and right! It's what God wants me to do. Because it makes me feel important! Because its big business and there's a lot of money in it. Because it's what I enjoy doing. Because I can't do anything else! It's what my dad did.)*

Whatever your reasons for wanting what you want, a good why will be consistent with who you are and what matters most to you. Every one of us has some underlying motive, reasons why we want what we say we want. Most of our whys serve to meet some need in us, which is no bad thing if our passions are noble and have the interests of others at heart. Those who struggle to find a noble and compelling why, live their lives without purpose, meaning and direction. Because their lives lack energy they never experience their full potential. Their contribution to the world is minimal. Such people wander through life wondering what to make of it and usually get involved in trivial pursuits. They live at a low level and are content to get by rather than get ahead. To escape the rut of existing but not living, they need to ask themselves a series of why questions to get to their fundamental why, and having done so, to settle on a why that will support what they want.

So not to get bogged down with the why question, it is important that you identify your fundamental why, and move quickly on towards what you want. The reason for this advice is that there is a tendency, especially in those who lean towards being introspective and those who are keen to do the right thing, to be unhelpfully self-critical. This tendency is unhelpful because it undermines forward movement and has you forever questioning the goodness and rightness of your desires, motives, reasons and actions. As long as doubt and uncertainty are allowed to go on in your head and in heart you will not be able to surge forward. Rather than do nothing because you are not sure that you have the right reasons for wanting what you want, it is better to begin your journey towards it, confidently, and to refine your attitude in the light of your personal growth. As you grow as a person, you will naturally want to re-affirm, strengthen and commit to your core values, principles, reasons and motives. This will help you to maintain integrity when moving forward and will ensure that you are not pulled out of shape by the demands placed on you as you reach to see your vision fulfilled. If what you want is good, give it your best and let the journey towards it make a better person out of you.

In your notebook, write down your fundamental why for the idea/vision you described yesterday? Is it a good enough why, a personal why, a compelling why, a why that is bigger than your personal goals and needs? Is it a why that has the well-being of others and the glory of God at its heart?

Motive Clarification

"Your hopes, dreams, aspirations are legitimate. They are trying to take you airborne, above the clouds, above the storms, if you will let them." William James

Week 2
Day 12 - How Comes After What and Why

 Because God's what and why were absolutely clear, it was not difficult for Him to decide on an effective strategy concerning how He would bring His will to pass in the earth. According to the Scriptures, God not only determined at the counsel of the Godhead, *what* would be, and *why*, He also determined *when* and *how*. By when and how, we are referring to how He would bring to pass in the earth what had been confirmed at the counsel of the Godhead.

The Scriptures have much to say about God's authority *over* the universe and His activity *in* the earth, summed up by the theological concepts: the Sovereign will of God and the Providence of God. By sovereign will of God we are referring to the doctrine that God's vision of the future will be carried out in the earth regardless of adverse circumstances, unfavourable conditions, uncooperative human beings and fierce resistance. The Word He has spoken over the earth stands and cannot fail to bring to pass His will in the earth. By Providence we are referring to the activity of God *in* the earth whereby He ensures the conditions that will facilitate His will being done. According to the Scriptures, God's how is based on His wisdom and foreknowledge. His foreknowledge allows Him to anticipate the future without the need to dictate it and His wisdom ensures that what He does or doesn't do or allows, will always be the best course of action, producing the best results possible.

Even though God knows all things (knowledge) He works out His will in the earth in very practical ways, (wisdom) taking into account human nature, sin and rebellion. Regardless of the opposition to His vision, God is able to use and fashion every event to suit His will. Nothing can thwart His vision of the future because what He wants and why emerge out of His divine nature.

Once you have come to a clear understanding of what you want and why, determining how to achieve it **must** come next. This necessary step in the creation of all things can be more difficult to define because how prompts us to move beyond talking about what we believe and want—the intellectual and emotional dimensions of a vision— to making it happen—wisdom. The how question forces us to bring things down to earth— it is intensely practical and volitional. How takes us, necessarily, outside of ourselves and among the daily realities of life where the circumstances are adverse, the conditions unfavourable, human beings unsupportive and the opposition to forward movement unrelenting.

Because how is often more difficult to determine than what and why, many have lowered their expectations and have settled for some lesser thing. They did this because they could not see *how* what they were wanting could be done or were unwilling to do what was required over the duration. They failed to factor into their decision to quit, the reality that new understandings, insight and opportunities are opened up to us with every forward movement, that *where there's a will a way will be made, that what you focus on you get, what you give off you attract. That the how you seek both exists within you, and has to be discovered, or outside of you, and has to be found.*

Although you and I lack foreknowledge and therefore cannot take full account of the obstacles that will present themselves along our path towards our vision, certain things are inevitable and are to be expected. If you and I are going to bring our unique contribution into the earth, there will be opposition, challenges, set backs, difficulties and resistance to overcome and to manage. Invariably, there will be things within you and things in your world that will resist change, progress and growth (Days 48 & 50). At times you will have to do battle with the thief in your mind that wants to steal your reason and the thief in the alley that wants to frustrate your vision. Jesus dealt with these two thieves in the garden of Gethsemane and with Peter. *(Luke 22:42; Mark 8:33).* So will you. As you walk out your how, your strategy, be prepared to go against the grain, to go the extra mile, to go it alone, just to rise above the pull of average.

It is also worth noting that God's great strategy, the great plan of redemption that He determined in eternity past, involved the sending of His

Son into an unfriendly and hostile environment to implement God's how. Contrary to expectations, God's how would not be a massive political and military campaign that would sweep away every opposition to His vision and usher in the **Kingdom of God.** Rather it would be a gradual, unassuming, unspectacular unfolding of the will of God in the earth. Your how will also have these features and contrary to what you might want, will be mostly gradual and developmental, rather than immediate and sudden. Too many people with a great what and a good enough why quit early because they did not reckon on how being difficult. They bought into the idea of being able to construct something of worth with the materials of nice and easy, safe and quick. Every compelling vision needs a plan, a method, a procedure, and a strategy to take us toward it. To build a great house, we must know *how!*

In your notebook, write down how you intend making what you have envisioned a physical reality. What immediate practical steps will you take?

Wisdom — Strategy

"Determine that the thing can and shall be done, and then find the way." Abraham Lincoln (1809 ~ 1865) *"When you know what you want, and you want it badly enough, you'll find a way to get it."* Jim Rohn

Week 2
Day 13 - A Definite Decision to Begin

To date we have learned that God knew what He ultimately wanted for the human being and for planet earth before He made a start (Day 8), had a clear picture of it (Day 9), could describe it in detail (Day 10) and had a why that was consistent with His divine nature (Day 11). Yesterday (Day 12) we concluded that He also knew how He would proceed to make what He wanted and why a physical reality. Once these important precursors of effective action had been determined, God made a definite decision to begin His work. He did this knowing that His vision for the human being and for planet earth would be challenged and that sin, suffering and death would mar His original design. He knew that their would be opposition to His vision to have the whole created order functioning in right relations to Him, knew that there would be threats from without, knew the risks involved in investing in the human being the power to decide and choose their own actions and knew that He would have to anticipate and manage the challenges in a manner consistent with His character. Still, He decided to make a start.

To decide to begin, especially when you know that there will be resistance and opposition to your vision becoming a physical reality, is no easy undertaking, but it is a necessary one. Which is why you will need to have a good enough why if you are to overcome the inevitable challenges that stand in the way of you acquiring what you have envisioned. Even God felt sorrow that He had made a definite decision to place a substantial part of His vision into the hands of the human being. *(Genesis 6:6)* Still, because He had a compelling what, a noble why and had made a definite decision to begin, He would remain true to His Word.

There comes a time in the life of every idea that a definite decision to begin is required. That will be the day that you decide to go for it. Once you know what you want and why, you have to begin your journey towards it, even though the outcome cannot be guaranteed and all you feel you need, in terms of resources, skills, support and favourable conditions have not been secured. The day you make a definite decision to begin will be the first day of the rest of your life. What makes that day a special day is not what is happening outside of you or around you, but what *has* happened within you. It is the day that you say to yourself, with conviction, confidence and credibility that from this day forward things will be different.

We are talking here about internal shifts in your readiness to take action. When this happens you know that you can procrastinate no longer, you cannot put it off anymore - the window of opportunity has to be now or you will be forever making excuses. These inner workings are powerful, for they herald the moment when you switch on your light, leaving yourself with only two choices: to be or not to be. What makes the moment of decision difficult is that the only thing that might have changed is your attitude; the external environment might not have changed one iota. There might not be anything spectacular about the day, no chain of events leading up to it, no celestial beings heralding the appointed time. More than likely it will be a day like any other day, nothing out of the ordinary to suggest that this is the day you have been waiting for and dreaming of. The only thing significant about the day is that it is the day you decided to make a start.

A definite decision to begin is the day you count the costs and accept the likely opportunities, frustration, set backs and challenges involved in turning a noble vision into its physical reality. It is the day that you say, "*I will commit to this vision even though I know that it will place a demand on my willingness to learn, change and grow.*" It is the day you decide to shut the door to your return to a life of ease, safety and comfort. A definite decision to begin is the day that you read the small print and decide that you will sign on the dotted line and will not change your mind. It is the day that you decide that you will put your hand to the plough and will not draw back. A definite decision to begin is the determination required to turn high-sounding words and great intentions into plans of action. Where there is no definite decision to begin, great ideas do not come into the earth. They remain in the realm of the intellectual and emotional— they can be described and talked about enthusiastically but never really enjoyed.

Like the notion of inside-out (Day 6) and the concept of how coming after what and why (Day 12), a definite decision to begin is the precursor of wilful and practical action. Many people find the volitional aspects of turning a dream into a reality to be the most difficult. But why, you may ask? What would stop someone from following through on an idea, thought, belief or goal that they have great enthusiasm for and a plan of action that is clear and coherent? According to the testimony of those who delayed taking action, *fear* was the debilitating emotion that rooted them to the spot. Fear of failure! Fear of success! Fear of criticism and ridicule! Fear of going it alone! The only way to fight fear is to act on your ideas, immediately and daily.

A definite decision to begin will take into account the possibility of failure, success, criticism and ridicule and being unsupported but will resolve to carry on, regardless. The day you decide that you will, not that you could or should, will be the day that your *will* gets involved in your idea. When this happens, forward movement occurs and momentum is generated. Until then the dreamer dreams on!

Make a list of the likely challenges and frustrations involved in your decision to take action on your idea. Include attitudes within yourself and in others and also the obstacles, difficulties, possibilities and risks involved. Consider each one squarely. Once you have done this make a written record of what you have decided to do.

Initiative — Fear— Resolve

"The most difficult part of any endeavour is taking the first step, making the first decision." Robyn Davidson

Day 14
Sabbath Week 2

Before I invite you to make your personal confessions of faith and to decide on this weeks' corresponding action, I want to summarise for you what we have discovered to date and how we might put them to work.

 God not only knew what He wanted (Day 8) and what it would look like before He had brought it into being, (Days 9 & 10) He also had a why that was consistent His values (Day 11). However, even though God had these prerequisites firmly in place, to translate His thoughts into action He required an effective strategy that could be worked on the ground, in very practical ways, taking into account the inevitable challenges (Day 12).

Once these important precursors of effective action had been determined, God made a definite decision to begin. Having made the decision to begin, God committed/covenanted Himself to seeing the vision through to completion and made a written record of His intentions. He had spoken and His word would be a binding and irrevocable oath. He had decreed and it would be carried out. He would be taking personal responsibility for bringing His word to pass (Day 2).

- Regardless of the opposition that would come against His vision, He would not be changing His mind or altering His Word/the written record of His will. He would be doing everything within His powers to make flesh the Word He spoke in the earth in eternity past.

 If we are going to bring into the earth the thing that we have conceived and nurtured from within, we must be clear about what we want and why and be able to see and describe it clearly. Once we are clear we need a series of corresponding actions that will move us towards what we want to see become a physical reality. These actions have to be worked on the ground, in practical ways, and ought to take into account the present physical reality—how things really are!

- Having got these things firmly in place, we must make a definite decision to begin and must commit ourselves to the work involved in bringing our vision to fruition.

I have conceived and nurtured from within a good idea, a noble thought, a godly desire that just might be my unique contribution to the world. Because of this, I make every effort to get clear about what it is and why I must do it, in order that I have a worthy and compelling vision for my life and life's work that God would be able to support.

I commit to spending time in the presence of God so that I might capture more fully His heart for what I believe He wants to do for others through me. I use my imagination to strengthen my conviction that what I have conceived and believed can be achieved.

I accept that to make what I see a physical reality I need to decide upon and carry out a series of corresponding actions that will move me towards what I want. I will do my very best to make these actions practical and will consistently apply myself to them. I make a definite decision to begin and I resolve today that I will put my hand to this plough and not draw back.

To take further the ideas of week 2, I will:

WEEK 3

Week 3
Day 15 - Beginning

Everything that God brought into being had a beginning, a starting point. The first verse of the first book of the Bible makes this emphatic in its opening statement: *"In the beginning God created the heavens and the earth. (Genesis 1:1 KJV)* Though He had thought about creating the heavens and the earth before they existed and had visualised, talked about and made a definite decision to begin it before beginning it, the universe would not be a wonder to ponder if He did not make a start. We would have no evidence of what He was thinking about and what He was capable of doing until He got started. To progress our ideas we must take action. This is what the Almighty Creator did. Once He had determined what He would do, He began in faith and took immediate action by beginning.

Beginning is an action that ***immediately*** follows a definite decision to begin. Once you have decided that you will, not that you would like to, the next step is to begin it at once, nothing doubting. Beginning is about taking the first few steps towards manifesting what you have conceived, enthused with passion and a purposeful why, envisioned and decided upon. It involves carrying out initial actions towards what you want to accomplish. Here is where a many people struggle. Beginning for many is difficult because, *"the journey of a thousand miles starts with a single step."* (Chinese proverb)

When you begin to take action on your vision, you are unlikely to have clear knowledge of how many steps will be required to get to what you want and the dates and times of the significant decisions, opportunities, challenges and experiences that await you. Perhaps if you knew beforehand what would be required: how many times you would be told, "NO!" how many others have tried and failed, how many doors you would have to knock on before you got a yes, how much you would have to invest before you saw a profit, you might not have begun. Which is why the advice of Dag Hammarskjöld is helpful, *"never measure the height of a mountain until you have reached the top, then you will see how low it was."* As many have found, beginning can be disconcerting because unlike your vision which you have enthusiastically embraced and nurtured from within, the vision has to be outworked in an environment outside of you, an environment that may be hostile, unreceptive, critical, adversarial, unsupportive and challenging.

Although the decision to begin is about resolving to see the process through, from beginning to end, before you journey up the mountain, what that journey will hold for you cannot be accurately predicted. No one can tell you specifically every detail about tomorrow— you have to walk into it, believing that it will be well with you. This is just how life is! The journey towards your vision begins with faith and proceeds from faith to faith. You set out believing that what you have decided to begin is good and worthwhile and that if you take certain actions, adopt certain attitudes and apply certain principles consistently, you will acquire what you are reaching for. But even this cannot be guaranteed. History is replete with examples of people who began well and achieved much, but not *everything* that they believed to see. This is no bad thing. *"If you shoot for the moon and miss, at the very least you will land among the stars."* (Les Brown)

Such people are not failures because they failed to capture everything they had envisioned. On the contrary, if the process has made them richer in spirit and in soul, they have obtained a far greater prize. Even though beginning does not inevitably end with completing; if you do not begin you will never know what might have been. You would never know what lie just outside of your starting.

Beginning is difficult for many because it requires a change of posture and a commensurate step of faith. Beginning is inherently about taking risks. To make significant gains, you have to make a start, even though success cannot be guaranteed. Even the smallest forward movement is premised on a willingness to take a risk. Take for example a toddler's first attempt at taking a few steps on its own. That decision carries the risks of falling, hurting themselves in the attempt, and the potential to experience disappointment, frustration and public humiliation. But the action has to be attempted and mastered if the toddler is going to progress to being able to jump, hop, skip and run. These higher order gross motor skills have a starting point; they begin with and are dependent on a 'definite decision to begin', (standing) and (a few first steps) 'beginning.'

If you and I are going to develop our full potential and skills and see the end of our faith, we must be willing to make a start. Regardless of the possibility that things could go terribly wrong, making a start also carries the inherent potential for greater achievement and success and the opportunity to experience feelings of elation and happiness, growth in confidence and courage. Success breeds success and fear breeds fear, which is why procrastination - the great thief of beginning - has to be resisted. Once you have decided to begin, make a start by carrying out a *few immediate* corresponding actions. *Immediate* actions will keep procrastination at arms length and carrying out a *'few'* corresponding actions will foster the momentum required to get you moving steadily forwards. Experience teaches that if you ponder the paths of your feet too long you will not be inclined to make a start.

Make a list of the things that prevent people from beginning. From your list, identify what has stopped you in the past. What might you do different next time?

Risk Management — Procrastination

"Whatever you can do or dream you can do, begin it. Boldness has genius, power and magic in it. Begin it now!"
Goethe

61

Week 3
Day 16- First Things First

Having made a definite decision to begin, God began immediately. He began with a clear measure of reality — how things really are— and with an action that would make the most difference to that reality. According to the Scriptures, *the earth was formless and empty and darkness was over the surface of the deep. The Spirit of God was hovering over the waters and God said, "Let there be light." (Genesis 1:2 NIV)* Notice there is no lengthy explanation of how things came to be this way, just a statement about the present reality. What follows is an action of the Holy Spirit that is tantamount to surveying a wasteland before deciding what action to carry out. When God said, *"Let there be light,"* He challenged the darkness, the reality of the present situation, and declared His intention to do something about it. The decision to begin with light was based on what the Spirit of God decided was most needful, because of what He had surveyed.

Rather than curse the darkness, God's first action was to do something about it. His was an assertive first action, a public announcement that He had made a start and that He would be taking other necessary actions on the back of His first action.

When beginning, it is good to first get a measure of how things really are, rather than why they are the way they are. Too many get bogged down with detailed analyses of how the present reality came about and in apportioning blame as to who is responsible for it. This type of questioning has its place, but it is not sufficiently helpful in moving us forwards. It dwells on the past rather than on the present and focuses on challenges rather than on opportunity. It is a problem-centred approach rather than a solutions-focussed approach because it keeps you wading in the deep for evidence and does not facilitate the light that is needed. A problem-centred approach is not a great motivator of action but tends to preoccupy and overwhelm the soul of the diligent.

Once you have carried out a cursory *reality check,* a survey rather than an inspection, you will have a good understanding of what your immediate action ought to be. Such an action would usefully be an action that announced your intention to the public, rather than some non-descript activity carried out in the safety and comfort of your study or closet. Too many people begin their enterprise with no increase in energy, passion, desire or activity. Fear and an unclear how might account for this. They shuffle papers on their desk, gather more information and more material to read and wait for the telephone to ring off the hook. What is required is direct activity rather than further deliberations. Without activity there can be no productivity.

Like the decision to begin (Day 13), the conviction of faith does not ignore what has happened in the past or the challenges of the present. On the contrary, faith is well aware of the hostile, unreceptive, critical, adversarial, unsupportive, challenging environment surrounding it. It's just that faith doesn't dwell on it. What faith does is give its best energies and focus to finding answers, opportunities and improvements, not from what has happened but within the opportunities of the present. It is the substance that brings about change.

Your first action is an important one for it is the action that sets you up to take other necessary actions. But why start with light? Without light the things created after the first day could not have been produced or sustained. Similarly without an assertive first action your next attempt will be predicated on the poor results of your first action and the results of your first action will shape the attitude behind your next action. For this reason it is good to begin strongly and to take the next action on the back of the first. An assertive first action is also required because going up against darkness, mediocrity and disorganisation will unsettle and expose the worlds of those who wish to live in ignorance. Such worlds are like strongholds; they do not yield ground readily, make every attempt to undermine and extinguish the entrance of light and thrive on intimidation. It is often the case that *"the people who oppose your ideas the most are those who represent the establishment that your ideas will upset."* (Anthony J. D'Angelo)

A good first action is primarily an announcement to the world that you are looking to effect that the way things are, is about to see change. It will not be a passive action, that cowers in the face of resistance nor will it be an aggressive action that fights fire with fire. It will be an action enthused with confidence. A good first action will be a positive statement of intent. Its aim and approach is not to curse the darkness and those who make a living out of it but to re-introduce the light. As a result, the darkness will be dispelled.

In your note book, write down how you could practical apply the principles of this study to an action that you have wanted to take but have not yet carried through.

Reality Checking — Corresponding Action— Assertiveness

"Better to light a candle than to curse the darkness." (Chinese Proverb)

Week 3
Day 17- Out of Nothing

 Although the Scriptures teach that God created, fashioned and made the human being out of material that existed before the human being, namely, the dust of the ground, the material that He used in creating the human being had a beginning— it did not always exist, that would make matter and energy eternal and only God is eternal. The Scriptures teach that there was a moment in the dateless past when God brought the physical material that the universe is made out of, out of nothing physical. He did this by the power of His spoken word, so that what we physically see was not made out of what can be physically seen. *(Hebrews 11:3)*

According to the Scriptures, when God first began His work of creation, nothing other than Himself existed. He had no pre-existing material to fashion and form into the universe. He had to call what did not exist into existence *(Romans 4:17)* and had to rely solely on His personal resources to bring His great idea into being.

 Sometimes when you begin to personally create something of value in the earth, you begin with yourself and the idea that you have nurtured and enthused, over these two qualities being the sum total of all that you have going for you. You have nothing more to work with! No resources, no support, no money, no supporters, no means, no way! This is when you have to pull out of you the faith required to bring what you need to you. Now it is true that the resources that you and I require to bring our ideas into the world already exist in the world. The money, the help, the resources, knowledge, plans, tools, people, skills, technologies you require is all around you. Because of this, there is no need to bring these into the world. What you need and perhaps lack is the means to get them to you, so that you can see, handle and make use of them. In this regard we are like God, beginning with nothing other than our faith and our burning desire (Day 5).

By out of nothing I am referring to the decision to make a start without the things that would naturally cause your desired effect. For example, you believe that you are called to pastor a church of 1000s but you do not presently have more than 10 people meeting in your living room each week. Or your vision is to run your own international company, but at present you are struggling to win the custom of local people. Or you have envisioned becoming a professional speaker but you are painfully shy and lack confidence because of a persistent verbal tick from childhood. Perhaps you have envisioned becoming wealthy but find yourself trapped and unhappy in a low paying job. Or you would like to travel the world, but fear flying. Or you would like to become renowned in your field, but no one knows who you are. Maybe you have envisioned becoming qualified in a field that requires entry qualifications that you are having difficulty obtaining. What is required in all these situations is a commitment to starting, without the means, resources, backing or skills that would logically facilitate your desired effect. But how is this possible? Through faith! Faith is the substance that is required to produce your desired effect. So what is faith? Faith is the conviction that although you presently lack what appears to be required, what you lack can be acquired, obtained, achieved even if you do not presently know how, through whom or by what means.

A look at the unlikely achievers in our world gives testimony to the fact that many people who have brought something of value into the earth, started with nothing more than faith in themselves and a passion for their product. Many were considered unintelligent because they did not complete their secondary education or had had an incredibly difficulty start in life, because of disability, poverty, adverse family circumstances. Even though many lacked the support and financial backing of major institutions and were ridiculed for their ideas, they overcame these challenges because they believed that what they could conceive and believe, could be achieved. Such people succeeded with a lot less than most. These people possessed the conviction, determination and energy of faith (Day 5) and showed to the world that all things are possible if you only believe!

So how does faith work? Because faith is rooted in personal conviction it provides the impetus and enthusiasm needed to attract what is required to get the job done and the determination to see the process of manifestation through to a successful end. Faith is demonstrated when we carry out commensurate corresponding actions towards what we have envisioned because we believe that it can be acquired. Just because what you appear to need is not presently in your possession, does not mean that it does not exist, cannot be found, obtained, acquired or made for you. Your faith will be the substance that will deliver what you want. It is the most effective agent for bringing something out of nothing.

In your notebook write down all the things that you feel are required before you could begin your idea. In light of what we have considered in this study, ask yourself whether you have enough to make a start. If yes, make a start, if not ask yourself whether anyone has started with less than what you have. I think you will find that others have done it, so why not you?

    Faith

"If I have the belief that I can do it, I shall surely acquire the capacity to do it even if I may not have it at the beginning."
Mahatma Gandhi (1869-1948)

Week 3
Day 18 - Beginning Again

 Genesis 1 has been interpreted by some as God beginning again after a cataclysmic cosmic event. We made passing reference to this in a previous study (Day 16) when we said there is no explanation in Genesis 1 of how the earth became *formless and empty, with darkness over the surface of the deep. (Genesis 1:2)* From what we know of God, this could not be His doing, for in Him there is no darkness and no void.

Whether or not your theological position is that something happened between verse 1 and verse 2 of Genesis chapter 1, making the creation narrative of Genesis chapter 1 an account of God reworking the charred remains of the earth into something new, Genesis 8 is a clear statement of God beginning again through Noah. Similarly, the redemptive work of Christ and the regenerative work of the Holy Spirit in the life of the believer speak of God beginning again with a new creation.

 Stepping out confidently is a beginning, (Day 16) but it is only a beginning (Day 15). There are many things along the path towards making your vision a physical reality that must be overcome, ensured, managed and avoided. We said that this was one of those inevitable facts of life when we looked at what should be taken into account when making a definite decision to begin (Day 13). Some of the things to be avoided will be attitudes and behaviours within ourselves; for example, arrogance and laziness (Day 48), and some of the things to manage will be external events that affect our personal world. Many people who are now doing something of worth in the earth had to summon up the courage to begin again. Perhaps after the death of a loved one, perhaps after redundancy, bankruptcy, ill health, a failed attempt, public ridicule and humiliation, a catastrophic event, for example a fire that destroyed all their work, a costly error in judgment, personal financial ruin, an economic down turn, betrayal by a business partner, a hostile takeover, withdrawal of funding. It takes courage to start again. Coming back from a major set back is no easy undertaking, especially if the fall was in public, from a great height and the result of personal sin. The reason why a fall in public can be difficult to handle is because failed attempts challenge our self-efficacy beliefs, attracts the attention of our critics and has personal consequences, which can take some time to unravel. Many in our world can speak of being overwhelmed by the emotional, physical, mental, spiritual, social, psychological, financial consequences of a failed attempt. Some have been unable to recover from the experience whilst others have lowered their expectations, vowing never to try anything of the sort again. Many now live different lives because of what happened.

Still, there are those who have picked themselves up to try again, albeit tentatively at first. History tells us that the path to success is littered with failed attempts, experiments and learning experiences. Those who view such things as mistakes and failures will have difficulty moving beyond them because repeated failure undermines self-confidence and has a tendency to erode self esteem and self-confidence. Those who move beyond failed attempts tend do so because they came to the view that, *"what looks like a loss may be the very event which is subsequently responsible for helping to produce the major achievement of your life." (Srully D. Blotnick)* Such people succeed in the long term because they promised themselves that they would never give up, that they would try and try again if they did not succeed at first and would learn, change and grow through the experience in order to succeed.

Unlike loss in personal confidence and the consequences of fall, the ridicule from our critics can be easier to handle if you remember that,

> *"It's not the critic who counts, nor the man who points out how the strong man stumbled, or where the doer of deeds could have done better. The credit belongs to the man who is actually in the arena; whose face is marred by dust and sweat and blood; who strives valiantly; who errs and comes short again and again. Far better it is to dare mighty things, to win glorious triumphs, even though chequered by failure,*

than to take rank with those poor spirits who neither enjoy much nor suffer much, because they live in the grey twilight that knows not victory nor defeat." *(Theodore Roosevelt)*

Even though recovery from a failed attempt can be difficult, it is not only possible but also likely, if you are willing to learn from the experience and to *'fall forwards'*. Experience teaches that difficulties tend to lose their power to hold us back if we show ourselves to be more tenacious and more resolute than the experiences of the past. Though it takes courage to begin again, to believe in yourself again, to learn from the past and to keep going, your definite decision to begin and your compelling why will help you through the difficult seasons of your life.

In your notebook, write down what you have learned and how you have benefited from the failed attempts, 'experiments' and 'learning experiences' of your past.

Learning from the Past— Failure

"Failure is simply the opportunity to begin again, this time more intelligently." Henry Ford (1863-1947)

Week 3
Day 19 - What Have You Got?

 God not only began with nothing when He brought the universe into being (Day 17), He also used the matter He brought into being out of nothing to create and fashion other features in creation. According to the Scriptures, He used the dust of the ground to fashion the human being and organised the chaotic, formless mass of raw potential to make the structures of the earth. More than anything physical, God used His individual genius to fashion the universe. By genius I am referring to His ability to make something wonderful out of nothing much. Had God not brought to bear on what He had available to Him, His ***individual genius,*** what He had available would have remained in their raw states. With God, what makes all the difference is not just the latent potential within a thing, which is the concern of today's study, but the use made of the thing by the person who handles it (Day 20).

 In a previous study we conclude that the universe that God created contains everything we will ever need for life and living on planet earth. God has already called these things into being and deposited in the human being the ability to make use of them. Unfortunately, most people do not avail themselves of what they have and are capable of because they are constantly in pursuit of what they think and feel they still need. What they fail to recognise is that the ability to fashion a good and productive life reside in the genius of each one of us and that what is required is that we take the raw materials of our lives and use them creatively to design and fashion a unique life.

When we speak of 'raw materials' we are referring to the personal resources, the experiences, abilities, capacities and skills that you and I are yet to make maximum use of. Much of this will be latent potential that must be awakened or under-utilised potential that needs to be developed, refined and intelligently directed. The secret here is not to discard or under-estimate what you have available to you. Whatever you have that is equivalent to the dust of the ground or a formless, disorganised, unclear mass of raw potential can be fashioned by your hands into something significant. Before you trample them under foot, make mud pies out of them and wallow in them, take a good look at what you can do, what you have experienced and been through, and what you know and are capable of. By taking a good look - a look of faith - you will see possibility where once you saw impossibility and you will be excited by a future yet to be designed.

If you were to complete an inventory of your life, to include everything that you have going for you and what you potentially have access to in the world, you would soon discover that you are immeasurably wealthy, because of the gifts and potential that God has uniquely deposited in the earth and in each human being. By the deliberate design of the Creator, much of what is in the earth is raw materials that you can take and do something unique with and raw materials that have been fashioned by human genius into something useful for others to appropriate. Each of us must take what we have and have access to, to uniquely design our life and life's work. This design process begins with recognising the potential within the raw materials that we all have access to and making effective use of the products, resources, services that have been brought into the earth through human skill and application.

So what have you got that could be put to greater use? If you have tried and failed in any way, you will have valuable experiences to learn from and to share with others for their benefit. Hurts, frustrations, misfortune, disappointment and challenges can all be transformed by genius into services. Whatever the learning experiences of your life, it is possible to *gather up the fragments of your life so that nothing is lost or wasted.* In addition to challenging past experiences, you have also accumulated knowledge from various sources over the years that can be put to good use. You have seen things, done things, succeeded and failed, loved and lost, laughed and cried. You have heard, read and learned from the success and failures of others. You have valuable experiences of what it means to be you – what it means to be young, old, black, white, rich, poor, male, female.

Do not despise the days of small beginnings and do not under-estimate who you are and what you have going for you. The capabilities of your physical body, the potential of your mind, the relationships you enjoy, the things you have experienced, can all work for you. The fact that you are still here shows that you have survived things that overwhelmed others and succeeded where some have failed. Regardless of the past circumstances of your life, you remain a resourceful and unique individual with much to share with the world. Before you go on a long trek in search of materials and resources to create with, or a good opportunity to jump all over, take a good look at the resources that you have within you and around you. If you put them to good use you should be able to use the resources of your present life to fashion a better life.

In your notebook, make a list of the 'raw materials' of your life that have the potential to be fashioned into more.

Personal Inventory — Self-Awareness

"Too often we underestimate the power of a touch, a smile, a kind word, a listening ear, an honest compliment, or the smallest act of caring, all of which have the potential to turn a life around." Felice Leonardo Buscaglia (b. 1924)

Week 3
Day 20- Utilising What You Have

We concluded yesterday that God used the dust of the ground to fashion the human being and organised the chaotic, formless mass of the raw materials of the universe to make the structures of the earth. If you and I were presented with the raw materials that God had available to Him we would probably make a clay pot and discard the disorganised, nondescript mass. But not God, He proceeded to make something beautiful out of them and brought out their fullest potential. He used His individual genius, the largeness of His thinking, to manifest His finest and best work.

According to the biblical doctrine of creation, what made all this possible was not simply the innate potential within the raw materials, but the *'pnuema'* that God breathed into every living thing He created. What makes the most difference is not the thing that a person has but the person who has the thing.

If it takes courage to begin again, it takes individual genius to do something unique with what you have available to you. By individual genius we are not talking about a formal measure of intelligence but the use of your creative potential and imagination to conceive good ideas that you subsequently take action on. Once you know what you have, it is up to you to make effective and full use of them. Now it is true that there is nothing new under the sun, that the thoughts you have some other person will have had them and that there are no new ideas just new arrangements. This line of reasoning should be of no consequence to you for two primary reasons. Firstly, not everyone acts on or fully follows through on their ideas. They either do not start or stop before the full potential of the idea has been realised. Secondly, the ideas that *you handle* will have your unique fingerprints on it. Though it may look like the ideas that other people have, there is a difference that no person can copy - the mark you leave on it. Until you personally do something with who you are, what you can do, what you know and are capable of, the potential within you and within the things that you own and have access to, will be untapped. Who you are at present, what you have and can do, can be organised, arranged and rearranged to facilitate a far greater purpose than the one you initially had in mind.

So let me ask you, if you were to bring your genius to bear on the ideas and abilities that you have, what would result? What could you achieve with your spare time, your loose change, your hobbies, your ability to smile, to love, to care, to speak, to write, to learn - if you got inspired? It is not what you have that matters most but what you do with it. Why not challenge yourself to make effective use of yourself and your resources, to dig into your creative potential, to do something wonderful for another.

This need not be costly in terms expenditure, it does however have to be unusual in the sense that not many people would think about doing it that way because it is outside the norm of how the masses think. This requires thoughtfulness on your part. So what could you do with what you have to enrich your life and the life of another? Usually you will have various options. The one you go for instinctively, out of habit, might not be your best and only course of action.

Take for example your loose change, what could you do with that? Answer: you could spend it, throw it away, save it, put it towards something else, give it away, or leave it for some unsuspecting person to find. By using your genius in this way, you will find that you could do a whole lot more with your loose change than what you have so far done with it.

The same is true of anything you have in this world. Why, for example, might two people with the same resources produce very different results? Why might someone attend a business seminar and increase their turnover by 80% within 6 months whilst another attendee produces nothing more? As we saw on Day 2 and Day 4 of week 1, we each must take responsibility for releasing and maximising the potential in good ideas. Rather than settle for an improvement in an area, why not go beyond that and become excellent and proficient, a master of your art. If you are going to unlock the full potential within your raw materials, you have to deliberately draw it out. So much more is possible, but you will have to exercise yourself to acquire it.

To make the most of what you have, the daily disciplines of practice, application, study, learning and change are necessary. To improve any skill, learning, whether on a conscious or unconscious level has to occur. By learning I do not mean being told what to do, nor do I mean being shown how to do it. Learning has come to mean more than that. It essentially includes the ability to carry out a new behaviour consistently, with increasing ease and proficiency - until you are unconsciously competent. To improve any skill we must apply ourselves to the process of learning, with particular regard to our learning intelligence - how we learn best. In practice this could mean modelling ourselves after a proficient person; reading books about the skill we want to improve; listening to audio-tapes about the skill; practising the skill and being able to talk our practice through with someone; observing ourselves using the skill, making changes that are necessary; learning the skill in a formal classroom setting or informally through role play. Whatever you know and can do, give them your best attention and the benefit of your ingenuity and they will become more in your hand.

In your notebook, write against each item on your list of raw materials what you could easily do to add greater value to the quality of your life and/or the life of some other. When you have done this, carry out the action and record the observed effects.

Individual Genius— Learning Intelligence

"Thou didst create the night, but I made the lamp. Thou didst create clay, but I made the cup. Thou didst create the deserts, mountains and forests; I produced the orchards, gardens and groves. It is I who made the glass out of stone, and it is I who turned a poison into an antidote." Allama Muhammad Iqbal (1877 - 1938)

Day 21
Sabbath Week 3

Before I invite you to make your personal confessions of faith and to decide on this weeks' corresponding action, I want to summarise for you what we have discovered to date and how we might put them to work.

 Once God had determined what He would do, He began in faith and took immediate action by beginning (Day 15). He began with a clear measure of reality — how things really are— and with an action that would make the most difference to that reality. His first action was an assertive action, a public announcement, that He had started to make changes and would be taking other necessary actions on the back of His first action. (Day 16)

- Although the Scriptures teach that God created, fashioned and made the human being out of material that existed before the human being, namely, the dust of the ground, the material that He used in creating the human being had a beginning— it did not always exist, When God began His work of creation He had no pre-existing material to form into the universe. He had to rely solely on His personal resources to bring His great idea into being. (Day 17)

- Once He had brought the dust of the ground and the formless mass of raw potential into being He used His genius to make something truly amazing out of them and brought out their inherent potential to the full. (Days 19 & 20)

- Because God is committed to His vision for the humanity He has repeatedly shown Himself as being willing and able to begin again. (Day 18) When His purposes were frustrated by the entrance of sin, He had an answer for it. His answer was an answer that would facilitate His vision becoming a physical reality - the sending of His Son into the world.

Once we have determined what we must do, we must begin in faith by taking immediate action. Our beginning should take into account how things really are and should be an assertive action, a public announcement that we intend doing something about the present situation.

- Beginning in faith is important because often we have to begin with a shortage of the things that would naturally cause our desired effect. When beginning we must make the fullest use of the things that we have access to and use our genius to do something unique with them.

- If we are committed to our vision we will be willing to begin again, should our first and successive attempts prove unfruitful. By learning from these experiences we enable ourselves to begin again, this time more intelligently.

I have determined what I must do, and I make a decision to begin it at once, nothing doubting. I know that the circumstances that I am likely to encounter will be challenging, nevertheless I begin with an assertive action, a public statement of intent, because I fully intend to do something about the way things have been.

I am willing to make a start without the things I thought I required, and will use the little that I have to great effect. Because I have made a definite decision to begin, I will not retreat. I am willing to begin again, should my first and successive attempts prove unfruitful. I will learn from my experiences and will keep moving. I believe that I will see the end of my faith and that I will reap if I faint not. I chose to 'fall forwards.'

To take further the ideas of week 3, I will:

WEEK 4

Week 4
Day 22 - Let Us

Creation is a collaborative work of the Godhead, not only in determination and design but also in its outworking. According to the New Testament, the Father, the Son and the Holy Spirit were involved in manifesting the Godhead's vision for humanity. This is implied in the creation narrative of Genesis when God says, *"Let Us make man in our own image and likeness." (Genesis 1:31 KJV)* The Scriptures teach that the Godhead had earlier met in counsel in eternity past to determine, among other things, the creation of the world, the permission of sin, the way of atonement and the consummation of all things.

The Scriptures also teach that each Person of the Godhead has a unique/lead role in the outworking of the Godhead's vision for humanity as well as being involved in the primary work of the other Persons of the Godhead. According to the Scriptures, God the Father is the *author* of creation, not exclusively but primarily; the Son is the *executive* of the Father's plan to recover the Godhead's original purpose for humanity (redemption), not exclusively but primarily and the Holy Spirit is the Person of the Trinity who *prepares* us to fit God's vision of the future, (sanctification). Not exclusively but primarily. Each Person of the Godhead supports the work of the Other, alongside their lead role in the divine economy of the Trinity, neither of them acting independent of the Other.

The let us concept when applied to ourselves is an acknowledgement that a truly outstanding work is a collaborative work, based on covenant relationships and partnership, respect for individual differences and a shared purpose to which each person is equally committed. The let us concept is an emphatic statement that no human being is sufficient in themselves and that each of us would benefit from the gifts, talents, abilities, aptitudes, skills, approaches, experiences, and knowledge that another possesses. The let us concept gives recognition to the abilities around the table and is a much better arrangement than attempting to go it alone.

Even when the vision of what you want is about your life and life's work, rather than a vision that involves others, for example your family, organisation, company, church, you act responsibly when you take into account the knowledge, skills, talents, wisdom, insight that God has deposited in other people. Without relationships, all you have available to you is what resides in you. Even though you are an incredibly resourceful human being, you will never be self-made. You are who you are because someone has taught you, showed you, helped you, listened to and made room for you. No man is an island! Even though *"many of us are more capable than some of us . . . none of us is as capable as all of us!" (Tom Wilson)* We all need relationships to become what we are capable of becoming. Unfortunately, in the strength of their eagerness some have ventured out into the great unknown, alone, without the benefits and covering of covenant relationships. What they needed and lacked were collaborative working relationships based on partnership, respect for individual differences and a shared purpose to which each person is equally committed.

According to the Scriptures, the Father, the Son and the Holy Spirit were relating to each other before they worked on creation. It was out of that relationship that they met in counsel in eternity past to jointly determine the creation of the world. The principle here is that whilst it is good to have a personal vision and to bring others alongside to work on it with you, it is better to jointly conceive and act on a vision that the good people that you are already know, love and trust can shape and own. Finding good people is more difficult than finding a good idea in the company of good people. The latter arrangement is advantageous because the essentials of effective teamwork, namely mutual trust, knowledge of and regard for each other, already exists. These things take time to develop and cannot be forced or manufactured.

Genesis 1:26 gives us another key principle of teamwork. In the verse, God the Father can be heard inviting the Other Persons of the Godhead to carry out, jointly with Him, their part in the work of creation according to what had been earlier agreed. What each Person of the Godhead contributed to the creation of the first human being is not made explicit in the Genesis narrative and is therefore not of primary importance. What is of primary importance is that they **together** brought the human being into existence. This principle of teamwork is an important one because the end result is credited to every person involved, regardless of what they individually contributed. There is no esteeming of one person over another because of what they contributed. As *Vince Lombardi* stated, *"the achievements of an organization are the results of the combined effort of each individual."*

For the let us concept to be truly meaningful it has to mean more than simply appreciating what others bring to the table. Let us is first about the inherent potential in close relationships and the opportunity to enjoy friendship, companionship, mutual trust, respect and support. Where such working relationships exist, there is less pretence and more open and honest communication. The let us concept works because it is fosters positive synergy - **T**ogether **E**veryone **A**chieves **M**ore.

In your notebook, identify how you work with others towards a common goal. Should you find that most of what you are working on is not with or alongside others, ask yourself why you have chosen/decided to go it alone.

Team Work — Partnership — Collaboration— Synergy

"Never doubt that a small group of thoughtful committed citizens can change the world; indeed, it is the only thing that ever has." (Margaret Mead)

Week 4
Day 23 - Who's Us?

The doctrine of the Trinity is a fundamental doctrine of the Christian faith. Simply stated, the doctrine asserts the unity of God (there is One) and the plurality of Persons in the Godhead, namely Father, Son and Holy Spirit. The Son and the Holy Spirit are represented in the Scriptures as being co-equal with God the Father in *'eternity', 'nature' and 'status.'* Thus, what we have in the divine economy of the Godhead, are the following: *1. unity, 2. equality of status, 3. an implied ontological order which is functional; 4. primary roles and responsibilities; 5. inter-dependence; 6. the absence of independent action* and *7. shared characteristics of deity.* These core characteristics of the Godhead provide practical insight into who to include and what to look for when putting together your let us team.

Unity is important because those who form part of your let us team have to be of the same mind and heart when it comes to the reasons why they have chosen to form and work as a team. What your let us team needs is agreement around the essentials (aims and objectives, purpose, values, beliefs, vision, attitudes) as well as being able to make room for differences of opinion, thoughts, ideas and approaches. The thing to avoid is people who are all the same in outlook. As we said about the Persons of the Godhead, they are the same in essence, but when it comes to the economies of redemption, namely how they have covenanted to relate with each other and the roles and primary responsibilities required to achieve their shared purpose for humanity, there is room for a degree of difference, which does not compromise the unity of the Godhead. What we need in our teams is unity within diversity. By unity we mean a shared vision, a common purpose that is shared and owned by people who are in covenant with each other. By diversity, we mean that there is sufficient difference in the team to allow for various sides, perspectives, views and opinions to be considered.

84

This allows blind spots in decision making to be covered.

Equality of status is about showing the same regard to and for each person around the table. Whilst there maybe a named person who is the public face of the team, organisation, church, family, company, as God the Father is in the Godhead, every person with a function is of equal importance to the team. Equality in its purest form resides only in the Godhead. Within the Godhead there is no esteeming of one person over another because of what they contributed. Even when particular recognition is given to one Person over Another, the involvement of the Others in the success of the Other is implied.

Related to the concept of equality of status is the notion that there is a *functional, ontological order* within the Godhead. By ontological order I am referring to the Scriptures that show Persons of the Godhead being in submission to Another, not because they are lesser but because it fulfils a necessary function in the redemptive purposes of the Godhead. We see in the Scriptures, that the Father is the 'figure head' of the Godhead, that the Son in His incarnate life is in submission to the will of the Father, takes His instructions from the Father and glorifies the Father and that the Holy Spirit proceeds from the Father and the Son, glorifies the Son and speaks of Him. There is no hierarchical arrangement in the Godhead. In organisational terms, the Godhead is a highly effective flat structure.

The implications for our lives of this principle is that it is right and proper for peers to defer to one another without either appearing lesser and subordinate and for their to exist among people the roles of captain, leader, director, chief executive, chairperson, pastor, husband.

As we considered on Day 22, each Person of the Godhead has a unique/lead role in the outworking of the God's vision. This principle teaches the value of allocating/delegating lead roles and primary responsibilities to members of the team. The value of this practice will be considered when we look at delegation and partnership (Day 44). As well as fronting a particular area of responsibility in the eternal purposes of God, each Person of the Godhead is involved in the work of the Others. According to the Scriptures, all things are *out of* the Father, *through* the Son *and by* the Holy Spirit. The value of this principle to our work is that no individual is left to carry out their own on their own, but is able to benefit from the involvement of others.

Related to this principle of partnership is the core value of accountability. By accountability I am referring to the absence of independent action. Within the Godhead, everything is based on interdependence– independent actions do not exist. Our organisations, churches, companies, families work best when there is consultation and the sharing of information and intention about a course of action. *"If a team is to reach its potential, each player must be willing to subordinate his personal goals to the good of the team." Bud Wilkinson.* Integral to the doctrine of the Trinity is the truth that the Son and the Holy Spirit possess the same characteristics of deity as the Father. This principle teaches that each member of your let us team ought to possess the same essential personal characteristics. Whilst the 'let us' concept hints at the value of working together, the benefits of working together depends on the characteristics of the team.

If you were to chose 10 people to make up your 'let us' group, who would you select, and more importantly why would you select them?

Group dynamics — Skills Mix — Legitimate authority

"Set your expectations high; find men and women whose integrity and values you respect; get their agreement on a course of action; and give them your ultimate trust." John Fellows Akers (b. 1934)

Week 4
Day 24 - Talking Answer

In a previous study we said that God had anticipated that His vision for humanity would not be without challenge or resistance and with this knowledge determined a plan, a strategy, in advance of the problem occurring. Not to prevent from happening everything that would frustrate His plan, but to maintain and redeem His plan in the midst of challenge. According to the Scriptures the mental activity in the Godhead when setting out the eternal decrees for our planet, also determined the involvement of the Godhead in the earth. The Scriptures teach that Jesus is the Lamb that was slain from the foundations of the earth. *(Revelations 13:8)* In other words, God had considered and provided in advance, a solution to the problem of sin. He did not spend eternity past thinking about how to avoid the problem of sin, rather He permitted it because in wisdom He knew how to use it and what to make of it.

When the entrance of sin was considered by the Godhead in eternity past, the answer came back, *"the seed of the woman will redeem the situation." (Genesis 3:15).* When the fact of man's rebellion spreading throughout the earth was considered, the answer came back, *"I will save a faithful remnant through Noah." (Genesis 8)* There is no challenge to God's vision of the future that He has not anticipated. God is a faith God - He believes in Himself and sees possibilities, opportunities and solutions in every challenge. He is also a great redeemer in that He is able to use failure, sin and human weakness to facilitate His will. With Him there is always a way out, a solution, and an answer of peace.

Talking answers is a solutions-focussed approach to dealing with difficulty. It involves looking at the inherent possibilities, opportunities, and solutions in a challenge. In this context, talking answers is an approach that a team or group might use to think through a necessary course of action that is fraught with difficulty or to address a challenge. Your let us team should be comprised of people who are committed to finding and talking answers. Such people are positive, resourceful, enthusiastic, committed, determined and creative. They are people of faith who will not use the vocabulary of defeat. They choose not use words like 'cannot', 'never', 'impossible', 'unlikely', 'improbable', 'maybe', 'perhaps', 'don't know', because they deem them unhelpful. Because they are people of faith, committed to finding answers, they will ask until they receive, they will seek until they find and will keep knocking until a door is opened. They are not the kind to labour long and hard over a problem but on the possibilities with the problem.

Because of their positive vocabulary and commitment to finding answers people of faith tend to find them more readily than those who give their heart and mind to debating the problem. People of faith are people who pray and do not faint. They will stay up late, carry out exhaustive research, will study, learn, think, explore and consult for as long as it takes to find a solution. They are not the sorts of people to keep digging the same hole to find different answers; they will try other avenues and explore other alternatives. They believe that where there is a will there is a way. These people behave this way because they believe that what they are working on is good and right and has the backing of the Almighty Creator. They have this conviction that they are on the right road and therefore likely to find answers on the way.

Such people are winners who do not know how to quit. They find ways where others make excuses. You will not find them using words - whether within or outside of their meetings - that pull down, nullify, condemn, criticise, or rubbish their ideas or the people generating them. Unlike *"followers who think and talk about the problems ... they think and talk about the solutions." (Brian Tracy)*. Such people use positive vocabulary to raise expectations and to create a different picture in the minds of those who have met to find answers; a picture that they are intent on making a reality. They use words purposefully and deliberately to tap into hidden depths and to draw out from these depths wisdom, insights, understanding and knowledge.

Together they make a winning team because they know how to take an idea and to build on it. They know how to draw out its full potential. Among the team will be those who offer occasional revelatory insight, people who prefer to think in silence, to reflect, to mull things over. Also among the team will be those whose individual genius is accessed through discussion with others, or through music and song, movement, visual stimuli, auditory stimulation, change of scenery, drawing, writing. Because these people are positive, resourceful, enthusiastic, committed, determined and creative they possess the qualities that are renowned for making things happen, for attracting what you need, for procuring what was out of reach, for manifesting what could not at first be seen. These people believe that there is tremendous power in the let us concept and that because of who they have around the table and the eternal significant of the issues being considered they can expect to receive answers of peace from the Father.

 In your notebook, identify the vocabulary, the emotional climate and the inter-personal dynamics between the people who are present at the meetings that you attend. How conducive are the meetings to finding solutions to challenges?

 Re-languaging — Perception — Possibility Thinking

 "Doubt sees the obstacles. Faith sees the way. Doubt sees the darkest night. Faith sees the day. Doubt dreads to take a step. Faith soars on high. Doubt questions, 'Who believes?' Faith answers, 'I'." Unknown

Week 4
Day 25 - What Do You Think?

 We know from the Scriptures that within the Godhead there is mental activity - a meeting of minds, the sharing of heart and conversations between them. This mental activity involves the intellectual, emotional and volitional aspects of God. The Hebrew words used to describe this mental activity speak of, 'to counsel' *(etsah)*, 'to take advice' *(sod)* 'to sit and consider together in deliberation *(niphal)*, to meditate, to have in mind, to purpose *(mezimmah)*, to be delighted in *(chaphets)*.

Without taking anything away from the omniscience of God, it is entirely consistent with the Scriptures to believe that within the Godhead there is mental activity. We know from the Scriptures that God knows all things, whether they are past, present or future, likely or actual, through one simple and eternal act. He knows all things, for all things were considered and taken into account at the eternal counsel of the Godhead. The purpose of the counsel of the Godhead in eternity past was not so that they might collectively come to know and understand through a process of discussion and learning, what will be and what they will do at such time, but to eternally decree it. This simple, eternal act occurred within the Godhead and could not have involved anything or anyone outside of the Godhead.

 Because you and I are not sufficient within ourselves as individuals and do not possess all knowledge, we must consult with various sources of knowledge so that we might know and come to better understand certain things. We might do this because the knowledge, skills, expertise that we need to shape and inform our thinking resides outside of us as individuals and outside the let us team that we have assembled. In these circumstances we do well to consult with people who have had significant experiences and success with the matters being considered. Such people will be masters of their art, will possess expert knowledge and skills in their niche area and will have many satisfied customers willing to attest to the help they have provided.

The people that you ought to bring alongside your let us team will have various approaches to providing assistance. Some will be consultants that you buy in, so that the team might benefit from their wealth of knowledge and experience of their subject. Some will be mentors who you speak with from time to time to help you think certain things through. Such people are there to help you make a decision, they will not decide for you. Some will be facilitators whose approach will be to draw out and bring to the surface the latent knowledge, skills, insights, answers, that exist within the team. Some will be master practitioner who you will want to bring alongside to share their skills. Others will be gifts of ministry to the body of Christ, people divinely appointed and endowed with spiritual gifts capable of moving you uniquely forwards.

Notwithstanding what these people have to impart, there is an infinite mind that ought to be consulted. The mind of God holds the unique answers that will move the team towards greater levels of success and well-being. According to the Scriptures, God makes His wisdom available to those who ask *(James 1:5)* and directs the paths of those who acknowledge Him in all their ways. *(Proverbs 3:6).* He presents Himself at their meetings, communicates His will through individuals and inspires the people mentioned above to impart His grace into the lives of those who are open and ready to learn.

To access the help of various sources of knowledge, one has to request it. Willingness to ask another for their thoughts, comments, help, advice and willingness to pay for it, is a major key to receiving the help needed. It is a rare and admirable attitude because it is an empowering admission of personal insufficiency, of having a learning need that you are willing to own and receive help with. The quicker you and I admit our need and shortcomings the quicker we will find the answers to meet that need. Many people are only too willing to come alongside another to provide them with help and timely assistance, but they wait their asking for it. Unfortunately, many struggle on in ignorance, because their arrogance and pride would not allow them to ask for help. Consequently they end up way of course -

confused and frustrated because they would not ask for directions, would not listen to advice, and would not submit their ideas to the scrutiny of friends.

Knowing what you want, who to ask and being willing to ask for it are the first few steps towards receiving the help you need. Everything you need is within you and needs to be drawn out or is in the possession of another and has to be requested. Do not be afraid to admit ignorance or to request help. If you are going to learn anything there needs to first be a recognition on your part that you don't know, secondly, acceptance that you need to know and thirdly, that there is information out there to know. You then need to be able to locate the source of information and once found, be able to evaluate its usefulness to your life.

 In your notebook, write down the names of the people whose counsel, advice, gift, knowledge, and opinion you regularly seek. How does each person contribute to your life? How have you benefited from what they had to say?

 Mentoring — Coaching

 "How different the new order would be if we could consult the veteran instead of the politician." Henry Miller (1891-1980)

Week 4
Day 26 - We Accord!

After the Godhead had concluded their deliberations in eternity past, they collectively agreed on what they had determined. Each had contributed to the deliberations and now each would be in covenant with the other to follow through on what they had agreed. There would be no independent action, no opposing views and no adversarial relationships. They would be acting and speaking as One. Everything that they had covenanted to do in the earth would be a collaborative work of the Persons of the Godhead, each Person supporting the primary work of Another.

Coming into accord with significant others around the essentials of operating a business, managing a company, enjoying family life or growing a church is an absolute must. It is an absolute must because two people cannot sing together unless they are in the same key. Among equals, agreement is often arrived at through frank and open discussion, much of which can be heated. Being able to identify and agree the essentials should be the desired outcome of your let us team, after the opinions, views, egos, beliefs, perspectives, interests, hopes and fears, wants and wishes, suggestions, comments, personal ambitions, values, ideas and thoughts of the members have been brought into the light. The aim of such a process is not to win everyone over to one point of view — the process is not about persuasion, coercion or manipulation, so that the voice of the more dominant members of the group is the only one heard. Rather, it is about inviting, weighing and judging every contribution for their respective value so that together we come to an understanding of what is right and best for the team.

As a process, coming to agreement can be emotionally draining, time consuming and personally challenging. Still, for all that, it is a better arrangement than having one person dictate the pace, direction and ethos of the group without involving others. A decision that is not shared or owned by group members, but reluctantly adopted and half-heartedly followed by them will not be effectively followed through. Deciding the norms of the group is that process of group behaviour where people get to determine and have confirmed the mission, core values and philosophy of the organisation. It is an important stage in the life of a group because it produces the essence of what is to remain after the details have been thrashed out. Thus, after much storming, jostling, posturing, arguing, discussing, deliberating, questioning, misunderstanding, upset and wounded egos, the team has arrived at its final position. What ought to follow is a clear and authoritative agreement that everyone can sign up to and own. Coming into accord about essentials is also important because it defines the boundaries within which the let us team will operate, lays out what is acceptable and permissible and what cannot be entertained, supported or approved, because it is inconsistent with what has been agreed. Coming into accord creates objective criteria so that every new member, thought, idea, belief, suggestion, direction is judged according to what is written *(logos)*.

Being a musical term, the state of accord is reached when distinct individuals flow together as one because each member tunes his/her instrument to the keyboard and chooses to follow the score. Once agreement around essentials has been reached and recorded (Day 30) what ought to follow is commitment to the agreement.

Commitment is an integral part of agreement because commitment has everything to do with following through on what has been decided. Those who feel unable to commit to what is written, or hold an opposing view should be asked to consider their position in the team. There is absolutely no value in your let us team taking decisive action on an idea about which there is strife, dissension, conflicts of interests, irreconcilable differences and discord. There has to be unity around the essentials if the team is to perform at its best. Without unity we have mutiny and without accord we have discord.

The power of group agreements is in the requirement that each person is invited to sign up to what is written. In some cultures this written agreement becomes a covenant, a binding agreement made between parties to carry out what has been agreed. These people become pledged to each other and to the vision of the team and agree to put the interests of the group above their individual interests. With commitment of this kind, *"nothing that they plan to do will be impossible to them." (Genesis 11:6)*

In your notebook, write down your response to this question. How committed are the members of your let us team to the objectives and core values of the team? How well do they relate to each other/work alongside other members of the team? How well do they handle correction, conflict, instruction, and discipline?

Covenant - Logos

"*Perhaps the most delightful friendships are those in which there is much agreement, much disputation, and yet much personal liking.*" *George Eliot (1819-80)*

Week 4
Day 27 - I Accord

 Yesterday we said that after the Godhead had concluded their deliberations in eternity past they collectively agreed on what they had determined. Each had contributed to the deliberations and now each would be in covenant with the other to follow through on what they had agreed.

As well as being involved in the work of the Other Persons of the Godhead, each Person of the Godhead was assigned a unique/lead role in the outworking of the eternal purposes of the Godhead. What that unique/lead role would be and how it would be carried out was determined at the counsel of the Godhead. What was required from each Person of the Godhead was acceptance of and commitment to the particular function that they would serve in the eternal purposes of the Godhead.

Being the executive of the Father's plan to recover the Godhead's original purpose for humanity (redemption), the incarnate Son of God carried out the will of God according to what had been decided. Even though it would cost Him His life, He stayed the course and fulfilled His part in the purposes of God.

 It is important to the success of your let us team that each member of the team owns and takes personal responsibility for carrying out their particular function within the team. Even though no one person can take sole credit for the achievement of a corporate goal, it is invariably the dedication of an individual working alongside others that brings home the glory for the team. Within every let us team there ought to be functions, roles and responsibilities that are assigned not to the team, but to one or more named members of the team. This is important because when everybody thinks somebody will do it, nobody usually does! Those that follow through will be people who have signed up with others to support the shared vision of the team. However, for them, signing up alongside others was not something that they did to save face or because they felt others expected it of them. They take the call to purpose more personally than that. Like others they are able to say, *"We agree to work together, to support each other to achieve our goal."* However these people have signed on the dotted line because they are personally convinced that the cause of the team is a noble and worthwhile calling.

Whilst others might be content to run alongside the pack, they have internalised the vision at a much deeper level. For them the vision of the team has become their life and life's work. These people are loyal to the shared purposes of the group and are similarly committed to playing their part in the grand scheme of the team. Though their part in the grand scheme of the team might be inconspicuous, the devotion they show to what they do makes it an indispensable act of service. If your let us team is to achieve its objectives it is not enough that members simply give verbal agreement/mental assent to what is being asked of them. Each person should be given the opportunity to state simply and straightforwardly whether they are willing to do according to what the team requires of them. This is important because the group needs to know where each person stands in relation to the core values and commitments of the team. This information enables the team to act and speak confidently and credibly with one voice.

Not only should teams strive for accord between team members (Day 26), each team member should also strive to come into full intra-personal agreement. Intra-personal agreement is a highly effective state of being for it enables individual members of the team to serve the vision of the team with the full support of their whole being. Where there is incongruence, intra-personal conflicts, people find it difficult to take action, because what they say, want, think, feel and do, are in conflict. There is warring in their members, which stops them moving confidently ahead. These internal struggles happen within the best of us when some aspect of our being has not fully embraced the vision and shows reluctance, hesitation, uncertainty, or reservation. Intra-personal agreement becomes stronger the more we give ourselves to, and follow through on, our worthy and noble cause. Consequently, intrapersonal agreement is revealed and refined by the fires of adversity. Simon Peter thought that he had given his all to the cause of Christ, when he said, *"Even if I have to die with you, I will never disown you." (Matthew 26:35, NIV)* Even the Son of God experienced a brief period of intra-personal conflict when He said, *"My Father, if it is possible, let this cup be taken from me. Yet not as I will, but as you will." (Matthew 26:39, NIV)* The difference between Simon Peter and Jesus is this: Jesus **willed** to follow through and brought His whole being into alignment with the will of God whereas Peter spoke out of one aspect of his person, his passionate emotional side.

It is human to feel stretched by a cause that places considerable demand on body, soul and spirit and to ask, *"Is the cause worthy of my personal investment?"* This is why, in your hour of personal challenge, you need around you your let us team, the people who are in covenant with you, so that they can confirm their covenant with you to watch and to pray. *(Matthew 26:36 - 45)*

In your notebook, identify the intra and interpersonal struggles that have made it difficult for you to take effective action/to come into agreement with other people. For example, "I have been hurt before." "I am not sure that I can trust them." "What if they take me for a ride?" " How have you/might you deal with these struggles?

Congruence - Cognitive Dissonance

"True love isn't so much a dreamy feeling that you have, as it is an enduring commitment to give sacrificially — even, or perhaps especially, when you don't feel like it." (William R. Mattox, Jr.)

Day 28
Sabbath Week 4

Before I invite you to make your personal confessions of faith and to decide on this weeks' corresponding action, I want to summarise for you what we have discovered to date and how we might put them to work.

 In the divine economy of the Godhead, every work of God is a collaborative work of the Persons Godhead, not only in determination and design but also in its outworking. All things are out of the Father, through the Son and by the Holy Spirit (Day 22.) Inherent in the divine economy of the Godhead are core qualities and characteristics of working effectively alongside and in covenant with others as part of a team. (Day 23)

- When in counsel together in eternity past, the Godhead anticipated and determined a plan, a strategy, before the challenges to their plan had happened. Not to prevent from happening everything that would frustrate their plan, but to maintain and redeem it in the midst of challenge. God is a God of faith; He believes in Himself and sees possibilities, opportunities and solutions in every challenge. With Him there is always a way out, a solution, and an answer of peace. (Day 24)

- Within the Godhead there is mental activity— a meeting of minds, the sharing of heart and conversations between them. We know that their 'meeting' in eternity past was a private meeting between themselves; it could not have involved Another. Because God is sufficient in Himself there is no need or lack in Him that would require Him to consult Another. (Day 25)

- Once the Godhead had concluded their deliberations in eternity past they jointly (Day 26) and individually (Day 27) agreed on what had been determined. Each had contributed to the deliberations and now each would be in covenant with the Other to follow through individually and jointly on what they had agreed. They would be acting and speaking as One.

 All truly great works will involve other people working alongside others in covenant. The benefits of working together depend on who is in the team and their attitude towards other members of the team. A winning team will have the hallmarks of the relationship that exists among the Persons of the Godhead and will be committed to becoming stronger in all areas.

- A winning team will be made up of people who are committed to finding and talking answers, people who are positive, resourceful, enthusiastic, determined and creative. People who do not engage in the vocabulary or behaviours of defeat but ask until they receive, who seek until they find and who keep knocking until a door is opened. If necessary they will bring others alongside, in order to find answers. Such people are not full of their own self-importance and will ask for help.

- When they counsel together there is a meeting of minds, the sharing of heart and conversations between them. The desired outcome of their deliberations, is agreement on what they will jointly and individually do, to carry out what has been agreed.

I recognise that a truly outstanding work is a collaborative work, based on covenant relationships and partnership, respect for individual differences and a shared purpose to which each person is equally committed. Because I am looking to produce an outstanding work and to live an outstanding life, I join myself with people who want the same for themselves and for others. I choose to join heart and hands with these people, as we work together for each other and for the cause that brought us together.

I will not jockey for position or recognition but will faithful serve others. I will support the work of the team and will welcome the support that is offered to me. I am willing to ask for help. I choose mutual submission over subordination and domination. I will not place my interests above those of the team. I choose to be responsible and accountable. I am a team player and will work hardest on myself so that I might serve the team well.

I will perform that which I have agreed and will protect the integrity of the team if I do not agree with a proposed course of action. Even though I am an incredibly resourceful human being, I acknowledge that I am not sufficient in myself. I am what I am because someone has taught me, showed me, helped and listened to me.

I choose to share with others the gifts that have enriched my life: -gifts of encouragement, enthusiasm, constructive feedback, support, a helping hand, a smile, a listening ear, patience, respect, honesty and faith.

 To take further the ideas of week 4, I will:

WEEK 5

Week 5
Day 29 - From Head To Hand

 Intelligence of the highest order was involved in the creation of the universe. The scientific formulas, laws of mathematics and physics that can be deduced from creation have engaged the minds of the brilliant thinkers of our world for centuries. Still, for all that has been revealed, discovered, understood and applied, there remains much 'out there' to know, and even more that cannot be fathomed or known. Included in God's great list of what cannot be fathomed are the billions of galaxies of the universe, of which our solar system is but one.

The whole thing was conceived in the mind of God. It was in wisdom that He designed and fashioned the Universe when in counsel with the Godhead. It was out of the gross wealth of His thoughts that He gave what He was thinking about a physical-spatial reality outside of Himself. It is therefore not surprising that the universe is a mystery - its Author cannot be comprehended either! He is fathomless! He transcends scientific analysis and experimentation, higher criticism and rational thought. No human being can have exhaustive knowledge of Him. However, even though what we know of the universe and its Author transcends us, we are able to enjoy, work with and use the laws of life to our advantage. This is because God is capable of translating the gross wealth of His thoughts into tangible physical reality. He makes His Word flesh so that we might have real acquaintance with His character and will.

 After you have talked together, deliberated, discussed, reasoned, considered and thought long and hard about an idea and have brought to bear on that idea the inclinations within the left and right hemispheres of the human brain, what ought to follow is a coherent way forward. In order for a group to benefit from its harvest of ideas, the discussion has to be more that an intellectually stimulating exercise that throws up new insights, understandings, knowledge, perspectives and more questions that require further discussion. To be of benefit, mental activity has to be translated into physical activity.

There is a tendency, especially if there are mostly reflectors and theorists involved in a team discussion and few activists and pragmatists, to overstretch the discussion with endless theorising, reflection, testing of hypotheses and alternatives, in order to come to a judgment. When this type of mental activity is not kept in check, groups tend not come to a definite decision about a course of action. Whilst the contribution of theorists and reflectors in group decision-making is an important one, it is not sufficient - there will always be something that cannot be known until action is taken. To avoid this tendency, heads and hands should be involved in the design and delivery of an idea.

If knowledge is to be of benefit it has to be made practical and tangible — it has to become actions that can be carried out. There is no understanding until knowledge is acted on! Where knowledge dominates, what results is an idea that is too complex and cerebral to implement.

The converse of that situation is no better. It would be unhelpful to allow the more creative and hands on members of the group to circumvent discussion by insisting on taking action without due consideration, thought or analysis. We all need each other to produce a well-rounded and comprehensive plan of action. A hands-on-approach that is not rooted in knowledge is a disaster in waiting. Equally, an intellectual exercise will produce nothing more than informed people, people who know a lot of good information but who are unsure about what to do with it and what to make of it.

To strike a balance between thinking and doing, a clear understanding of the relationship between wisdom and faith is required. Wisdom is valuable because it invites us to consider things through before taking action. Wisdom is practical, rather than intellectual, and must not be confused with rational procrastination— the justifications of inaction. Wisdom is a necessary safeguard against foolishness that is often labelled as faith. Faith on the other hand is not about doing things that do not make sense; it does not involve believing and taking action on things that are unreasonable, illogical or absurd. Faith is about taking definite action because a person has grounds to believe that the action is the right one to take, even though they do not yet know whether it will actually prove to be so.

Whilst faith is required to translate a good idea into an action, wisdom is required when determining and carrying out the action. No matter how earnest and fervent our faith, faith will not get an idea off the ground if the idea was not designed and built to fly! This is why we need good heads, good hearts and good hands to manifest a good idea.

In your notebook, summarise how decisions are made and plans of action agreed in your let us group. Is there conflict between wisdom and faith, between thinkers and doers?

Thinking Skills - Whole Brain Thinking

"Ideas must work through the brains and the arms of good and brave men, or they are no better than dreams." Ralph Waldo Emerson (1803-82)

Week 5
Day 30 - It Is Written

We know from the Scriptures that the Godhead met together in counsel in eternity past to establish what would come to pass in the earth. The main topic of discussion at this 'meeting' concerned the eternal purposes of God for the new species of being that would inhabit the earth. In theological terms, the meeting involved, foreordaining, purposing, covenanting and pre-determining Creation, the Permission of Sin, the involvement of the Godhead in the world, namely, Providence; the Provision of Salvation and Judgement.

Once the Godhead had decreed what would be in the earth, they agreed a 'written record.' The Judeo-Christian Scriptures we refer to as the Bible is a written revelation of the outworking of the purposes of God for the human being. In effect, the Bible is the Word of God, the 'summary of the minutes of the meeting' of the Godhead in eternity past. Consequently, it is the final authority over the planet.

Like the One who spoke over the planet in eternity past, the Scriptures are an infallible, living and active, authoritative, forever enduring revelation of God. They came to be in our hands because God spoke to, moved on, influenced and 'carried along' the writers of the Scriptures and preserved an ample written record of the outworking of His purposes in the earth.

We said yesterday that our meetings and discussions ought to conclude with a clear, coherent and definite plan of action, a strategy that takes us out of our heads and puts the idea firmly in our hands so that we can do something with it. Like the Judeo-Christian Bible, the plan of action should have the following features. *Firstly*, it should be written so that we have a permanent, accessible, legible and historically accurate and confirmed record, that people can read, make references to, quote and consult. It should also be written so that people are able to operate from document - *"it is written"*, rather than from memory or the oral tradition - *"can anyone remember what was said?" Secondly*, it should state the reasons, circumstances and purposes for which it was produced. *Thirdly*, it should be dated, as this will confirm its historicity, give extra weight to its universal nature and its ability to be relevant when faced with changing circumstances and new challenges.

Fourthly, it should bear the names and the status of the people who were involved in producing it. This will give the written record a personal touch and link it to people known to the group rather than to unknown individuals. The inclusion of names and status on the document will also add credibility and give it authority. *Fifthly*, it should be esteemed as a significant and authoritative document so that everything is judged against it and anything that conflicts with it disregarded. *Sixthly*, because it is an authoritative document, it should be consulted in planning and decision-making. As the document will be the result of the mental activity of thinking people and hands on people, (Day 29) it will be well thought out and thoroughly researched document that interprets itself. *Seventhly*, it should be produced in summary and widely circulated so that everyone who comes under its influence can be familiar with its core values and statements.

Eighthly, it should be taught to all who come under its influence. *Ninthly*, the document should be talked about continually so that people do not let slip from their lives its core values and statements. *Finally*, it should be preserved and kept safe; defended, loved, delighted in, respected, kept in remembrance, grieved over when men disobey, hid in our hearts, hoped in, meditated on, rejoiced in, trusted in, obeyed, spoken of and esteemed as light. It should be conformed to, entreated, obeyed and used against the enemies of our purpose and plan.

The above outline of the important features of a strategy document can be applied to any work or endeavour, whether produced by an individual or team. For the individual, it is useful to have a written document that was produced on the day that they got clear about their life and life's work. Similarly, for families it is helpful to have a document produced from discussion, which captures the core values, goals, aspirations and commitments of the family. The same ideas apply in business, in ministry, in church life and in organisational planning.

Though God is Almighty and know all things, He operates from document. The Bible teaches that God in eternity past recorded in the volume of the Book things concerning His will for the Messiah *(Hebrews 10:7)* and acts in the earth according to His Word. He does things by the Book!

In your notebook, write a mission/vision statement for your life and/or life's work. Remember to include the features mentioned, where applicable, and to involve others in the process if they are likely to come under and be affected by the document.

Logos — Strategy Document— Mission Statement

"My aim is to put down on paper what I see and what I feel in the best and simplest way." Ernest Miller Hemingway (1899-1961)

Week 5

Week 5
Day 31 - Planning Your Work

 We know from the Scriptures that God in His sovereignty determined from all eternity whatsoever will come to pass in the earth, and works His sovereign will in His entire creation, both natural and spiritual, according to His predetermined plan. A plan based on the foreknowledge, wisdom and goodness of God and the collective counsel of the Godhead. According to the Scriptures, the plan of God is the premise for the Providence of God and facilitates the eternal purposes of God. The Providence of God speaks of God's involvement in the created order, whereby He upholds, preserves, works in and through, and directs all things to their appointed end. It is about how what God has determined will come to pass in the earth, through whom He will do what He has determined, when they will do it, how it will be done, where and why.

The Scriptures teach that the plan of God concerning humanity is both decretive and permissive. It is decretive in that the pivotal, eternally significant events of our world are not left to the will of the creature to determine, whereas other things are. The majority of the things that happen in our world are within the permissive will of God - things that are allowable because they have little bearing on His eternal purposes for the planet. The things that are decretive are the main features of His plan, the significant milestones, goals and objectives that He decreed in eternity past. These things are not left to the will of the creature.

The plan of God is also developmental - it has a definite beginning and a definite ending. In between the beginning and the ending is a mix of remarkable and unassuming events, the significance of which can only be understood from the vantage point of God. Because the plan is based on the wisdom and foreknowledge of God and is facilitated by the Providence of God, problems have been planned for and the consequences of human error, rebellion and disobedience have been anticipated. To the untrained

111

eye, the wisdom behind God's who, what, where, when, how and why can appear ridiculous, at best paradoxical. However, because God knows all things, and is good, what He has in His sovereignty willed for creation will always be the best course of action, producing the best results.

 When planning your work it is important that it proceeds from your vision (Days 9 &10) is consistent with your mission statement (Day 30) and the things that you consider to be fundamental to your life, family, church, ministry, organisation. (Day 26) Your plan will be the blueprint, the pattern that has to be deliberately followed to achieve your desired outcome. It will be a series of corresponding actions that you expect will manifest your vision of the future. A good plan will map out the length and breadth of your vision and will be comprehensive and coherent. It will have a definite beginning (Days 15 & 16), a middle and an ending. It will take into account the law of process, which states that what you want is unlikely to manifest all at once, but will proceed dynamically - gradually and suddenly. Because what you want will unfold dynamically, patience and discernment are required.

A good plan will outline what needs to happen and the stages and the steps towards the completed picture. It will have anticipated the inevitable challenges along the way and will have formulated an adequate reply. It will be inherently practical and will give particular attention to *who will do what, where, when, how and why.*

It will come from the heads and hands of your let us team and will be an organised and intelligently directed plan of action. It will not be a rigid, inflexible plan of action that tries to cover all eventualities, as heads alone would have it, but a flexible plan of action that ensures that important and necessary things are carried out and that other things are allowable.

Because good planning often precedes effective action, we do well to take care of things that can be anticipated in our planning, this gives us confidence to handle the unexpected, the things that could not have been anticipated. Because we see in part and understand in part, our plan will reflect our present knowledge and understanding. As we work our plan it will be necessary to change some detail, to revise, clarify, alter and amend the plan in light of our having a better understanding of the end from the beginning. Even when we know what we want, knowledge alone will not produce anything until it is organised and intelligently directed through practical plans towards a definite and worthy end.

In your note book, identify one of your short/medium term goals and devise an action plan that includes the 5WH approach, namely who will do what, when, where, how and why. Where possible, include other concepts from day 31.

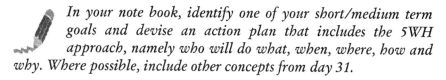

Action Planning - Problem Solving - 5WH Approach

"The reason most people never reach their goals is that they don't define them, learn about them, or even seriously consider them as believable or achievable. Winners can tell you where they are going, what they plan to do along the way, and who will be sharing the adventure with them." Denis Waitley.

Week 5
Day 32 - SMART Goals

 God's thoughts are organised and His plans intelligently directed. Because of this, He does not act sporadically, impetuously or on a whim— He knows what He has in mind when He releases His creative potential. Every action is deliberate and effective. Because God knows specifically what He wants as an outcome and what will be required to produce that outcome to His timescale, He is able to make measured judgments about whether it has been achieved.

We see this SMART (**S**pecific, **M**easurable, **A**ctivity, **R**elevant and **T**imescale) procedure played out in the creation narrative of Genesis chapter 1. Each day has an objective, a goal, a desired outcome that is stated simply and specifically and each day has an action, some activity that would bring about God's desired outcome for that day. In the Genesis narrative that action is God speaking His desired outcome into being and fashioning the human being from the dust of the ground. Each action of each day is a relevant action, in that it relates to God's desired outcome for the week. Furthermore, each action is begun and completed within a definite timescale, at the end of the day, which means that God is able to compare what He had in mind with what has come into existence.

According to the Genesis narrative, God was able to 'sign off' each day's work because what resulted was what He wanted.

 There are many approaches to planning action. The 5WH method we considered yesterday is inherently practical and captures well the main features of a plan of action. However, when combined with the approach we are considering today, the SMART approach, the 5WH method is systematised. The SMART approach focuses specifically on the objectives of a plan of action and how they might be achieved. The SMART approach. By specific we mean that the objective can be clearly stated - it is specific, definite, unambiguous and unequivocal. It is not a general statement of intention that is difficult to define and measure but a clear statement of expectation. The notion of being able to measure achievement of a goal is a valid one and speaks of being able to assess, gauge, quantify the impact of relevant activity on an objective within a given time period.

There are many distinct advantages to setting SMART goals. SMART goals provide positive direction because they are specific. SMART goals focus on results and enable plans to be made and work to be prioritised and organised towards achievement of the goal. SMART goals give purpose to activity and focuses concentration and attention. Because SMART goals involve the undertaking of relevant activity, they reinforce self-efficacy beliefs by feeding back that relevant activity has had an impact. They provide both intrinsic and extrinsic rewards, which are powerful motivators of consistent action. SMART goals also explain and justify effort and action, attracts the support of others because they are deliberate and measurable and have a definite outcome in mind.

Integral to the SMART approach are the skills of time and project management. These skills help us to effectively organise our work and ourselves so that we intelligently deliver our desired outcomes. To deliver our desired outcomes economically and on time we often have to organise and prioritise our work, mobilise people and resources to help with some aspect of the work and manage people, resources, the process and ourselves until the outcome has been achieved. Whilst achievement of a desired outcome is our primary goal, to do so efficiently, on time, in an organised and intelligently directed way, is far better than achievement that has cost more than what was required.

In your notebook, use the SMART approach to organise another of your short/medium term goals. Remember to be specific, to include quantifiable milestones so that progress can be measured and relevant activity within a realistic timescale.

Time Management— Project Management

"The goal you set must be challenging. At the same time, it should be realistic and attainable, not impossible to reach. It should be challenging enough to make you stretch, but not so far that you break." Rick Hansen

Week 5
Day 33 - The Power in Doing

As we saw on Day 31, the Providence of God speaks of God's involvement in the world, whereby He upholds, preserves, works in and through, and directs all things to their appointed end. It speaks of the *activity* of the Godhead in the unfolding purposes of God for the planet. The Providence of God involves each Person of the Godhead doing what they had agreed to do in the earth when they met together in eternity past. It is because of the Providence of God that the will of God will be carried out in the earth. The Scriptures teach that God does not leave the details of His plan for the planet to be determined and carried out by some other, but works His will in His entire creation, both natural and spiritual, according to His predetermined plan.

His plan is not a wish list, nor is it a record of what He would like— it is an action plan that He owns and unfolds through relevant activity. According to the Scriptures, God performs relevant activity through the release of His Word. He is a doer of His own Word and does according to what is written (Day 30). The Universe would not be ours to enjoy if God had kept Himself to Himself and said nothing. It would not be and we would not exist! All things would have remained hidden in Him and unrealised. We would never know Him, what He was capable of and what He had in mind if He did not act on His thoughts. Similarly, we would never know His amazing love if He did not send His Son into the world to carry out His will towards the people of the earth.

What you and I are capable of will benefit no one until we *do* something with all that we have within us. Potential is not enough, it has to be intelligently directed outwards so that what is possible can become an actual physical reality if others are to benefit. Some things will just not happen for you until you make them happen for you! Fortunately, there is tremendous power in doing, especially for the human being. Which is why God gave the species of being He created in His own image a physical body - so that we act on and make things happen in our physical environment. As human beings we produce by doing; create by doing; make things happen by doing. We harness, unite and direct the powers of our mind, emotions and will when we do. We change and cause things to change when we do. We accomplish by doing. We discover ourselves by doing; learn by doing; acquire and develop skills by doing. We have new experiences when we do; find things out when we do; release our potential when we do. Doing fills our day with meaningful mental and physical activity. It enriches our lives and gives us something to talk about with others. It is better to do something than nothing; better to do than to think about doing, to talk about doing, to observe others doing. Doing requires a change of posture, action and movement. It is an act of the will.

Doing is extremely important to the quality of our human experience. The breadth of the human experience teaches that those who do nothing or little become idle, inexperienced, underdeveloped, staid and unaffected. They become ineffective and unlearned people, ignorant of life and lacking in physical vitality. They lack vitality because doing releases more energy to do more. It has a rejuvenating effect! Those who do nothing tend to also speak critically about most things. They are quick to criticise and quick to pass judgment on those who are attempting something. They are quick to laugh at mistakes and at those who are trying their hand at something different. Those who do nothing go nowhere and try nothing, live very dull lives. Because they lack mental and physical exercise, challenge, and the joy of achievement they tend to have frequent periods of ill health.

In contrast, those who are having a go, who are keen to try their hands at something new, develop themselves in so many areas of their life. They are ever learning, changing and growing and take responsibility for the outcomes of their life. They do not sit back and wait for things to be brought to them — they show initiative and take action. They do not wait to be affected and influenced: they affect and influence! They are the innovators and inventors of our world. Such people learn from their mistakes and try again and again if they do not succeed. They are skilful with their hands and tend to become masters in their art. They do and keep doing until they become excellent. They discover new worlds of possibility and opportunity every day because they are willing to take a look, to push against the doors of life to see what is on the other side. They are curious people who have a love of life. They test themselves all the time. They are not the kind to do for doing sake— they are not restless spirits, nor do they shy away from thinking. Theirs is relevant corresponding activity.

By relevant activity we mean that what they do relates to where they are going and by corresponding activity we mean that their actions are based on thoughts, plans, ideas, conversation and thinking. Such people act intelligently: and are very effective in achieving outcomes. Though they tend to be results orientated, they are not overly task centred. They are too busy doing what works, what matters most and is of value and of benefit to be distracted from their work. Because they work SMART they are not involved in feverish activity that has them chasing their tails. They know that haste undermines effort.

In your notebook, make a list of the things that you do on a weekly basis and make judgments about the type and value of the activity. Ask yourself, is what I am busy doing: productive, intelligently directed, relevant, corresponding, thoughtless,s wasteful, peripheral, trivial, ineffective, hurried, feverish, pointless, necessary, helpful. This will give you a stark picture of the reality of your activity.

Corresponding Activity - Personal Power

"Start by doing what's necessary; then do what's possible; and suddenly you are doing the impossible." Saint Francis of Assisi (1182-1226)

Week 5
Day 34 - Doing What You Do Best

 Yesterday we discovered that the Providence of God speaks of God's involvement in the world whereby He upholds, preserves, works in and through, and directs all things to their appointed end. A more detailed understanding of the Providence of God shows the activity of each Person of the Godhead in the unfolding purposes of God and what they individually initiate, facilitate and accomplish in the earth. We said as much in a previous study when we concluded that each Person of the Godhead was assigned a unique/lead role in the outworking of the Godhead's vision for humanity at the counsel of the Godhead in eternity past. (Day 22) Consequently, we see throughout the Scriptures each person of the Godhead carrying out their particular function in the divine economy of the Godhead.

In the Old Testament we see Jesus Christ, the Son of God carrying out the Providence of God towards God's covenant people Israel. A closer look will find Him carrying out 'duties' and 'prerogatives', 'tasks' and 'types' of His Incarnate Work — the work He would be doing as a human being to execute the eternal decrees of the Godhead in relation to Salvation. Similarly, we see in the Old Testament the Holy Spirit appointing, anointing and empowering people to carry out their part in the eternal purposes of God.

Although there can be no suggestion that each Person of the Godhead was allocated a role based on what they would do best, what we can usefully deduce from our analysis is that each has a particular function in the outworking of the purposes of God in the earth.

 To accomplish the shared vision of your let us team it is important that each member knows and feels at ease with what each person brings to the table by way of knowledge, skills, interests and talents. To get a measure of the personal skills and inclinations of your let us team, it is worth asking each member questions that identify what they enjoy doing. For example, *what do you have enthusiasm for? In what ways are you intelligent? What comes easy to you? What are you good at? What area of service would be both a joy and a challenge to you?* Once you know what that place of service is, you will have found the key that will open the door to that person's usefulness, contribution to the world and to the team. What you then want to do is to create opportunities for them to develop and become excellent at what they already have an inclination toward.

Because potential flows outwards, it has to be intelligently and commensurately directed. There's nothing more frustrating to a tremendously creative person than being in an environment that stifles creativity and makes no room for what they are good at doing. It is an unbearable pain, the sort of pain a great thinker would experience if it they were to spend 8 hours a day on an assembly line, doing the same activity over and over and over again, week in and week out. There's no greater motivation to releasing potential like doing what you enjoy doing and are good at. In fact people tend to be good at the things they enjoy doing. Such things come out of their natural desires, passions, personal strengths and skills.

Thus, to make significant progress as a team, each member should be allowed to play to their strengths and to put effort and energy into what they do well. Each one should then strive to be faithful and effective in their niche area, for the good of the team. By niche area I mean the area of service and place of contribution that would allow them to give their best, to pursue their passions and interests, to grow and to excel. Finding one's niche area is important because it is the optimum environment for the release of your abilities and enthusiasm. In such an environment we are innately motivated to invest time, energy, emotional interest and commitment. Unfortunately, too many people lack the determination and application required to excel in what they are good at and many are stuck in positions that are outside of their skills set or below their ability range. As a result they feel unfulfilled and frustrated in their personal and professional development.

Once you have found your place in your niche area it is important that you give it your best on purpose. This will involve learning all you can, reading all the books you can, acquiring and developing your skills set, increasing your knowledge and meeting regularly with people in your line of business in order to learn from and contribute to what is excellent.

Each of us possesses skills, intelligences, personality attributes, mental and physical abilities and talents that can become more in our hands. We must not allow ourselves to remain in positions or on career ladders that do nothing for the enlargement of our spirit. We were made to excel! Neither should we allow ourselves to be grounded by comparison with another person's abilities, by low aim or by our own or other people's fear of heights, change and new things. Rather, we should strive for mastery and excellence in at least one area of intelligence, for ourselves and for each other.

In your notebook, write down what you would like to spend your working week/your business day doing, if you had the power and freedom to design your week? How similar is it to what you currently do each week? What could you do to replace your current working week with the one you would choose for yourself?

Skills Inventory - Multiple Intelligence

"If you have a talent, use it in every which way possible. Don't hoard it. Don't dole it out like a miser. Spend it lavishly like a millionaire intent on going broke." Brendan Francis

Day 35
Sabbath Week 5

Before I invite you to make your personal confessions of faith and to decide on this weeks' corresponding action, I want to summarise for you what we have discovered to date and how we might put them to work.

The will of God concerning the earth was conceived in the mind of God and determined at the counsel of the Godhead. In wisdom God designed the Universe and in wisdom He translated the gross wealth of His thoughts into a physical-spatial reality outside of Himself. Intelligence of the highest order was involved in the creation of our Planet. (Day 29)

- Once the Godhead had decreed what would be in the earth, they agreed a 'written record.' The Judeo-Christian Scriptures we refer to as the Bible, is a written revelation of the outworking of the purposes of God for the human being - a record of the implementation of the 'minutes of the meeting' of the Godhead in eternity past. (Day 30) God now works His sovereign will in His entire creation, both natural and spiritual, according to that written record. The record is a based on the foreknowledge, wisdom and goodness of God and the collective counsel of the Godhead. It includes how what God has purposed will come to pass in the earth, through whom, when and how. (Day 31)

- Because God's thoughts are organised and His plans intelligently directed His words never fail to accomplish what they were spoken to accomplish. He acts systematically and on purpose and every action is deliberate and effective. (Days 33, 34) He knows specifically what He wants as an outcome and brings it all about within His pre-determined timescale. (Day 32)

A truly great work will involve a meeting of minds, the sharing of heart and a pooling of resources around a shared goal. The outcome of the meeting of minds ought to be a written plan of action that is practical and coherent, one that can be intelligently implemented. The plan should detail who will do what, when, where and how and should lay out specifically what relevant activity will be required and a realistic timescale for each to be achieved.

- The actions required to progress the plan should be allocated to team members based on their gifting, skills, abilities, knowledge and strengths, so that each bit of the endeavour is placed in competent and enthusiastic hands.

I understand that a truly great work will involve a meeting of minds, the sharing of heart and the pooling of resources around a shared goal. I also understand that the outcome of such a meeting ought to be a written plan of action that sets out who will do what, when, where, how and why. I appreciate that it is not enough to have a written plan of action and that relevant activity and a realistic timescale within which to operate is required.

I understand that if the vision the plan outlines is to be achieved, necessary actions have to be effectively carried out by all concerned.

Because I am keen to see the vision that we have conceived together become a physical reality, I will be quick to do what I am required to do and will support others in doing what they are required to do, so that each bit of our endeavour is implemented effectively. I share my knowledge, skills, talents and abilities with the team and I strive to be excellent in all my undertakings.

To take further the ideas of week 5, I will:

WEEK 6

Week 6
Day 36 - Building By Design

God builds by design and works all things both natural and spiritual in the earth according to His predetermined plan, a plan based on the foreknowledge, wisdom and goodness of God. Building by design is what God also intended for the human being in the earth. His will was that the human being would use the tremendous powers He placed within them to make the rest of the earth like the Garden of Eden and the whole earth like the Kingdom of Heaven *(Genesis 1:28)*. Working in and through the human being remains God's primary and preferred method of building by design. He still looks for and works through human 'contractors' to bring His will to pass in the earth. People who chose each day to build according to His pattern, rather than by their own imaginings, preferences and will. Presently, God's primary agent of His unfolding purposes in the earth is the Church, people who have set aside their own ambitions to build according to the design of the Author and Finisher of the Faith — the Lord Jesus Christ.

Unfortunately, much of what has transpired in the earth since our unique creation has involved the use of our human resources to erect 'buildings' that transgress the will of God. The world we know and live in is not entirely the world the Creator intended. Rather, it is the world that we have created by the choices we make and the laws of life we break.

Once you have planned your work (Days 31, 32) you need to work your plan, on the ground, with others, in the real world. There must come a time in your planning when you leave the drawing room and step outside your office to do what is required to make the drawing a physical reality. It is not enough to enthuse over an idea that has been captured in print, you have to do it! *"**You can't build a reputation on what you're going to do.**"* Henry Ford (1863-1947) Action is required. As we have discovered, there is tremendous power in doing— it is doing that we turn our ideas into their physical reality (Day 33), especially when we do what we are good at (Day 34), have enthusiasm for (Day 5), alongside and in covenant with others. (Day 26) Alongside and in covenant with others is a necessary feature of building by design — outside of covenant each person is free to add their own features to the building, to build according to the vision in their own eyes, to be self seeking and competitive.

Building by design is a fundamental concept of the construction industry. It speaks of the requirement to work from a blueprint and takes effect when co-operation and mutual respect is shown for the work of the architect, the site manager and the contractors. The work of the architect is to draw out the plans for the building, the work of the site manager is to supervise and direct the work as it is being carried out, so that it reflects the design of the architect, and the work of the contractors is to build according to the drawings of the architect and the onsite instructions of the site manager.

Whilst your enterprise may not require the specific roles of architect, site manager and contractor, it will require that actions are carried out in a manner consistent with the decisions reached and the plans agreed in counsel with members of your let us team. Ideally, and this will depend on the nature of your enterprise, heads and hands will have been involved in the design and development of an idea (Day 29). This allows each person to experience and have respect for the design process and for the various roles and functions that facilitate the end product. Many organisations have not been able to build by design because their senior management team, the people charged with drawing up the plans, were too far removed from the people who make it happen on the ground. Frustrated by this some senior managers have resorted to authoritarian leadership styles that are coercive and dictatorial. What they fail to realise is that the best way to build by design is to work alongside the people who make it happen on the ground so that they see in the behaviour and enthusiasm of their managers the intelligence of their blueprint and the value and relevance of their work.

Depending on the work you are engaged in, it is sometimes necessary to bring alongside your let us team people who will work with you to make the vision of the team a reality. These people will be 'sub-contractors.' So that they also build by design, the additional people you bring alongside should be inducted into the team's way of working and be given the opportunity to hear the vision and to see the plans of the architect. Building by design does not mean that what has been decided has to be exactly followed through, when better judgement and new information suggests differently. It is often only by working our plans that we find it necessary to change, revise, clarify, or amend some detail. Building by design ought not to be exact or exacting, particularly if your work is about ideas, people, learning and change. Unlike your mission/vision statement, (Day 30) your action plan (Days 31 & 32) is a working document that can be altered to reflect the work that is under construction. This can be done without having to also alter your mission/vision statement. To build by design, the 'logos' drawings of the architect have to be frequently consulted and the internal 'rhema' voice of your site manager acted on.

In your notebook, write a brief summary of how faithful you are at following through on the promises you make to yourself. How careful are you to do what you have said?

Corresponding Activity - Parallel Planning – Logos - Rhema

"You don't just stumble into the future. You create your own future." Roger Smith. "Every man is the architect of his own fortune." Appius Claudius (4th century BC)

Week 6

Day 37 - Building On The Previous

The notion of building by design is further developed by the idea of building on something done before. Not only does God build by design, according to His predetermined plan, His work of creation was rolled out day by day over a period of a week. Once God had brought forth light, He brought other things into being that would be dependent on light. God's first action was a 'foundational' first action, a public announcement, that He had begun, and that He would be taking other necessary actions on top of His first action (Day 16). God's next action complemented the first and each successive action built on the one that came before it. This process reached its height when what God had in mind from the start, the human being, was created on day 6. Everything prior to the unique creation of the human being was made to support and benefit the human being. What we have outlined in the Creation narrative of Genesis is an ecological relationship, a process of interdependent stages that can be reduced to discreet parts that can be separately measured and evaluated. (Day 32)

When each of the days of Creation are put together what we have is synergy at work, where the sum of the whole is greater than the sum of its parts. Even though God's present activity in the earth appears to lack the momentum, order and coherence apparent in the Creation narrative, His will continues to be carried out in the earth according to His action plan and timescale for the planet.

Building on the previous is first about establishing a good foundation upon which everything else will come to rest (Day 16). Once the foundation has been laid, what is required is that we build by design, one brick at a time until the desired height is reached. Because building on the previous is about building incrementally, over time, it is important that each phase of your enterprise is not hurriedly finished. In eagerness to complete and move in, some have decorated and furnished their buildings before the plaster had time to dry! In effect, they took short cuts that were to prove costly in the long run. In the construction industry we have independent people, third party organisations and regulations to prevent this sort of thing from happening. We often need similar people and systems in our lives, people and procedures that keep us accountable, so that we build well and right. When building any enterprise it makes sense to do things by the book, even though building by the book might slow the whole thing down by weeks and months. Because people are the primary building blocks in the vision we have for family, church, organisation, enterprise, ministry, it is important that we handle each one with care.

Building on the previous is also about gaining momentum and leverage on our work. It is about getting maximum benefit from the actions and energy that got us to where we are at present. Rather than separate individual acts, unrelated to anything before or after, building on the previous recognises the value of putting together a good run, so that each action sets us up for the next and the next. It is about working with the next stage in mind so that we are able to fluently and seamlessly move into it. This is really important. Many promising ventures were started but not finished because nobody thought about what should come next.

Rather than build on the back of a successful sale, some became complacent and lost the momentum needed to keep going. Instead of formulating a game plan for the next ten years many slept through the day only to awake in the evening not knowing what to do next. As a result they lost momentum, failed to get leverage on themselves and had to start again.

As we build a brick at a time, faithfully doing the few things that make all the difference, it is important that we do not allow ourselves to become discouraged by what seems like another day of doing the same things over and over again with little noticeable change. As we show ourselves faithful to the task at hand, the day inevitably comes when one more of the same causes us to break through into another level. Everything prior to that action was meant to prepare and set us up for the manifestation of our finest and best. Then, when the moment of manifestation arrives the whole thing surges forward. A corner has been turned and it is time to reap the rewards of sustained sowing. Though it may have taken you what seems like a lifetime to fill up your cloud, your faithful sowing will produce the harvest of your life. Due season waits!

In your notebook, review the major events of your life and organise them in a way that is meaningful to you. Can you see any patterns or recurring themes? Is there momentum, order, process and coherence? Does any of it make sense? Can it be understood? Can you see the law of cause and effect, of sowing and reaping at work in your life?

Leverage

"Look at the stone cutter hammering away at his rock, perhaps a hundred times without as much as a crack showing in it. Yet at the 101ˢᵗ blow, it will split in two, and I know it was not the last blow that did it, but all that had gone before." (Jacob A Riis)

Week 6
Day 38 - Formative Evaluations

 At the end of each working day, period of activity, God made a productivity judgment — He came to a definite conclusion concerning whether what He wanted to accomplish had been achieved. According to the Creation narrative of Genesis, God looked over the work of His hands and concluded that it was *'good'*. It was judged to be good because it looked everything like how He wanted it to look. By deeming it good, God, in effect, 'signed off ' the job. What we have outlined in the Creation narrative of Genesis is a description of God carrying out a series of formative evaluations of the work under construction. Each day is separately measured and evaluated before God proceeds to the next phase.

Because the process of Creation is made up of independent stages it was necessary for God to build on the achievements of the previous day. (Day 37) Each job had to be successfully completed because the next task was dependent on it. At the end of the 6th day God considered all that He had done and concluded that it was ***very good (Genesis 1:31).*** He was able to come to this summative judgment (Day 52) because His formative evaluations had given Him a measure of the end result of all His activity.

 The practice of periodically evaluating our activity is an essential feature of planning SMART (Day 32) and of building on the previous (Day 37) As we work our plan and see what we have imagined take shape and gather momentum in the earth it is very important that we remain true to our core values and core business. (Day 44) When enthusiasm is not intelligently directed we tend to get caught up in the momentum of activity to the extent that we no longer take time out to deliberately and periodically check our efforts against our first criteria. The buzz and excitement of realising ones growth potential (Day 45), of seeing your building being raised up, has to be tempered by quiet reflections and critical evaluations so that we do not lose sight of what matters and become complacent.

To keep us rooted to what is true we must regularly evaluate ourselves and our work against objective measures. Before beginning the next stage of our endeavours it is sensible to assess and make productivity judgments about the discreet piece of work, project or job we have just completed. This is important. If there is a fundamental flaw in a previous job, the flaw will undermine the entire building. This is why it makes sense to 'sign off' each bit of our endeavours as God did for each day of creation. Without periodic, formative evaluations, productivity judgments whilst a work is in progress, most things get off track, sometimes dangerously off track.

Periodic checks on route ensure that we know where we are in relation to where we are heading. They are tantamount to taking a break on a long journey so that we can refresh ourselves and confirm our direction and progress on route. These checks are very important because they present us with an early opportunity to consider our ways and to make mid course corrections. They provide us with direct honest feedback. Without this feedback we wander off course without realising it. Many great starters have lost valuable time because they walked in a particular direction for years before they realised that they had gone off on a tangent and were now way off the mark. If they had taken the time to regularly review their lives against their success criteria they would have known where they were going and where they were likely to end up if they continued down the same road. They would have been able to quickly turn their lives around.

Periodic checks are similar to anti-virus systems on a computer— they keep our lives free from clutter and scan our operations for things that could undermine our work. We all need systems, arrangements and people in our lives that help us to maintain a pure walk towards our vision of our future. These arrangements, though challenging, give us time and space to remove the weeds from our garden before they take root and choke the good things that are spring up around us. It would be foolhardy to run our lives without these things in place. Only the arrogant and the complacent operate without checks and balances. Because the Word of God, like the drawings of the architect, is most effective in providing rebuke, correction and instruction in

134

what is right, *(2 Timothy 3:16)* it makes sense to habitually sit before it with a willingness to change when challenged.

How often you carry out interim checks will depend on what you have decided in your SMART plan of action (day 32). Some things have to be checked often, perhaps at the end of the day or at the end of the week, because every hour counts and the issues are of critical importance. Other things can be checked less frequently. What is important is that we habitually create space in our lives to evaluate, to check and confirm progress and to learn from what we have done. Though critically examining a work in progress is unsettling, it is better to check your work on an ongoing basis than to wait until the end. Waiting to see whether the structure is sufficiently robust to support the roof and cope with the destructive elements that will inevitably come against it would be foolish. It is better to make changes now whilst the work is in progress, and can be corrected, than wait until it is completed.

In your notebook, carry out a formative evaluation of an area of your life/life's work. As you critique that area of your life/life's work, it is important to identify and celebrate your successes and to acknowledge areas for improvement.

Success criteria

"If I've got correct goals, and if I keep pursuing them the best way I know how, everything else falls into line. If I do the right thing right, I'm going to succeed." Dan Dierdorf.

Week 6
Day 39 - In Your Image

The Scriptures teach that the human being is a unique species of being, created in the Image of an Awesome God, who imagined and created us deliberately and uniquely for Himself. *(Psalm 8:4; Revelation 4:11)* It is this distinguishing feature, being created in the image of an invisible God that connects the human being to the divine Being. As God is our Creator and was involved most intimately in our unique creation, it should come as no surprise to us that the human being would have features and characteristics that resemble the Person of God. The laws of genetics lends support to this notion, but differs in this regard, our likeness to God is not in our physical composition but in our soul— our ability to speak, to think, to imagine, to decide, to choose, to know, to understand, to act. Similar to us, the heavens and the earth also reflect the Person of God. The heavens declare the glory of God, show His handiwork, speak of and for Him *(Psalm 19:1-2)* and reveals His eternal power and divine nature. *(Romans 1:20)*

As a result of being created in the image of God, we are also like Elohim in that we are capable of taking a thought, a desire, an idea, from our fertile imaginings to manifest the physical reality of that thought, desire, idea - a physical reality that will inevitably and eventually come to resemble our dominant traits, interests, desires, ambitions, fears, aspirations, moralities and character. As the dominant species on the planet, human beings possess great power to influence and change things, to effect and transform our environment. Consequently, each of us builds according to the quality of our personal being. Thus, much of what has transpired in the earth since our unique creation is the work of the will of the human being. The world we now know and live is what *we* have created.

What you are working on and investing in will eventually come to resemble the quality of your personal being, as it will take on your dominant traits and will reflect your values, emphases, priorities, predominant attitudes, approach, style, manner and character. There's no getting away from this law of life. Your work will reflect you! You are the architect of your own fortune; the one with the greatest influence on your ideas. The one who decides what your ideas and life will eventually look like. Similarly, the ethos, philosophy and culture of your working environment, company, church, family, organisation is created by you, if you are the one with the greatest influence over the minds and lives of the people within them. This is why you must model right attitudes and behaviours if your work is to be honourable.

The psychological process we are describing is not one that should be forced or manipulated. The process is about the quiet influence that one person has on another. Those whose influence is considerable and charismatic, must be careful that they do not use the influence of their personality and the authority of their position to stifle, distort, reduce, truncate what is unique and different about people. Your job is not to replace the personality of those who come under your influence, so that they think, speak, present, act and dress like you. It is not about filling the earth with another you! Regardless of how good you think you are, you are not that good! Rather it is about allowing and helping each one to become what God has uniquely deposited in them and destined for them.

Because your work will reflect the dominant characteristics of your person, it is important that you work hardest on yourself by becoming increasingly like Christ. The will of God concerning your life is first a call to Christ-likeness and secondly, the making of Christ-like disciples.

One of the distinguishing features of an effective person is their commitment to personal improvement. Such people take seriously their personal growth and are ever learning how to realise and fulfil their personal and leadership potential. They have an insatiable appetite for personal development, strive to be good people, place character above personality, virtue above achievement and people above projects. They are always looking for ways to be and do better and tend to encourage the same spirit in others without ever demanding it. Such people recognise the importance of putting first things first, which is why their first concern is to order their private lives and to consistently experience personal victories - daily victories over their own thoughts, feelings, habits, attitudes and domestic circumstances. They recognise that they must live what they believe and model what they also want others to know, learn, do and become.

Such people are good students of progress and potential and are keen to put into practice what they are learning. They positively welcome honest feedback and are open to receiving counsel, instruction and comments from those who see things differently. They do not see themselves as having arrived but as having much to learn. They see themselves as students first, not authoritative teachers - disciples not Masters. Because of their humility, enjoyment of learning and commitment to the process of becoming, they are a pleasure to be around. They are in touch with their own humanity and with the humanity of those they seek to influence. Because their influence is benevolent and aspirational, rather than autocratic and manipulative, the people around them tend to show the same good attitudes and behaviours in their lives and work. When this happens they have successfully produced after their kind.

In order to attract people of quality and to manifest your finest and best work, it is important that you commit to becoming a better person. Whatever you want your people to be, you have to, at the very least, be that to them! Whatever you want your work to look like, you have to model. It's not what you say, nor is it what you do that has the greatest influence on the people you lead, who you are as a person carries the most weight and speaks the loudest.

In your notebook, answer the following. In what areas of your character development are you weakest? What affect is it presently having on others around you/on your work? What could this area of personal weakness cost you publicly if left it unchecked?

The law of expression - The law of accumulation - The law of cause and effect

"Every man's work, whether it is literature or music or pictures or architecture or anything else, is always a portrait of himself." Samuel Butler (1612-80)

Week 6
Day 40 - Put Life Into It

Having formed man from the dust of the ground, God breathed into what He had formed the breath of lives (plural) and man became a living soul. *(Genesis 2:7)* According to the verse, the physical thing that God had fashioned with His hands did not become a living soul, a complete and fully functioning being, until God breathed the breath of lives into it. According to the account, God enthused the thing that He made with the fullness of His life. He did not hold back in investing Himself in the human being. Nor did He simply speak the human being into being as He had done previously with the other living things. The creation of man is different. In the Genesis narrative the involvement of the Godhead in the creation of man is not implied, it is stated- *"Let Us make man in our own image and likeness (Genesis 1:26).* Being the crown of God's creative activity in the earth and the last thing to be fashioned, it is not surprising that God would invest so directly and intimately in the human being. God involved Himself directly and intimately with the human being because He had destined the human being to act in the earth according to His will and to be the dominant species on the planet.

As God's supreme representative in the earth we see Jesus applying the same principle of personal investment to His work. Throughout the Scriptures we see His unreserved investment in the will of God, an investment that would require Him to freely give His life, not just metaphorically but literally. As a result of His considerable personal investment in a worthy cause, a great work was accomplished.

The principle of personal investment is extremely important if we are going to produce a great work. While it is possible to create something in our image by just being around it often enough, for that thing to truly become us we must give of ourselves to it, deliberately. With the former, the person who you are effects things without deliberate effort on your part - through osmosis and association the thing comes under your quiet influence. However, with the latter, the influence you exert is deliberate, conscious and purposeful. Similarly, your best work will be produced by giving it everything you have got. If you are going to produce a great work you cannot simply rely on others to **catch** your spirit, you have to invest yourself in them. Your good idea will become your finest and best work to the degree that you give it your all. By all, I mean that you ought to give it your time, attention and affection. You have got to invest your best physical effort, your interest and enthusiasm, the powers of your mind, will, emotions and spirit and the resources of friendship, time and money to the idea. It has to become your 'meat and you drink.'

Once again we are talking about a healthy obsession, not a fire of dangerous passions that rages without internal control or self-management (Day 5). It would be counter-productive to exhaust yourself physically, emotionally, mentally, spiritually, socially and financially by investing everything at once in pursuit of a worthy idea. You would simply burn yourself out before you got near to it being realised. Which is why it is important that you enjoy rest, a good nights sleep, time spent in leisure, on holiday, with family, in prayer and that you have other interests.

By investing personally in your work you are insuring yourself against laziness and indifference, in yourself and in your team. Many people would like to produce a great work but their level of personal investment is minimal. They are happy to have others invest their lives in **their** work, and may even demand that they do, but with regards to their own investment, they would rather supervise that work and wait to reap what others have planted. This type of attitude will not produce a great work, for as we saw yesterday, people will not be inclined to give, to do, to follow, to work for another if they do not see in the other a readiness to give, to do, to follow, to work.

It is often the case that your finest and best work will not be the first thing that you have invested in. Sometimes your greatest work, your masterpiece, the thing that you will be most proud of, manifests once you have mastered the skills and the disciplines required to produce that work. This is understandable; even though you are enthusiastic and committed, you have still much to learn and to understand. It takes time to get everything in place, but once you do and preparation meets opportunity, your finest and best will be realised.

If you have found the thing that will be in your bosom like a burning fire, you will naturally want to give it your best. So let me ask you: *"are you bored with life? Then throw yourself into some work you believe in with all your heart, live for it, die for it, and you will find happiness that you had thought could never be yours."* Dale Carnegie (1888-1955)

 In your notebook, write down what you would be personally willing to do to manifest your finest and best. What have you already done?

 The law of inertia

 "Give your dreams all you have got and you'll be amazed at the energy that comes out of you." William James.

Week 6
Day 41 - Working The Laws Of Life

Who better to model your work of creation on than the Creator of the Universe? It was for this very purpose that *Principles of Creation—Manifesting your Finest and Best* was written - to show you how God manifested His finest and best work and how you might manifest your own. My intention was to draw your attention to the general principles and processes involved in Creation and how you might practically and usefully apply them to you own work of creation, personally and vocationally.

To help us come to an understanding of God's method of operation in Creation, His *modus operandi,* we began each day with an introduction to an idea, concept, principle or strategy from the Biblical account of Creation from the vantage point of the Creator. After which we examined the implications for our own work. The reason behind this approach was to show you that the modus operandi of the Creator in creating the universe are the principles of creation for how life works best. God not only formulated these laws, He works His will in the natural world by them. In fact the whole of nature operates according the eternal laws of God. *(Genesis 8:22) "Even though what we know of the universe and its Author transcends us, we are able to enjoy, work with and use the universal laws of life to our advantage." (Day 29)*

So what are these universal laws of life and how might we work with them to our advantage? One such law is called *the law of cause and effect (Day 1).* This law states that if there is an effect - some outcome, result, phenomena, condition, it was caused — something or someone made it happen, whether directly or indirectly, consciously or unconsciously. This law is also called the law of seed time and harvest, because we all get to reap what we have deposited in the earth. Another law, ***the law of faith (Day 17)*** is the most fundamental of all laws. Simply stated, the law of faith states that if you believe you can, you can and if you believe that you can't, you can't! Thus, all things are possible to those who believe! The law of faith asserts that just because what you want is not presently in your possession, does not mean that it does not exist, cannot be found, obtained, acquired or made for you. Another law, ***the law of expression, (Day 6)*** states that you are what you eat, or in other words, whatever is impressed into your mind is also expressed into your reality and becomes your reality. So if your life is not to your liking, take a good look at what you are listening to, who you are spending most of your time with and what they are sowing into your mind.

Another of the general laws of life is ***the law of control, (Day 2)*** This law asserts that if you take responsibility for your life, the circumstances of your life and the results of your life, you are more likely to succeed than if you wait for a good opportunity to find you or for some other to make it happen for you. ***The law of accumulation (Day 37)*** states that wherever you are in your life right now is the result of the ideas, experiences and people you have accumulated in your life. ***The law of concentration (Day 9)*** states that you get what you concentrate on, commit to and make your focus and ***the law of inertia (Day 33)*** states that you lose what you don't use!

Another law, the ***law of attraction (Day 39)*** asserts that, what we have in our lives we have attracted because of the person we are and that we draw into our lives the information, circumstances and people we need in order to carry out our dominant thoughts. The law of attraction explains why some people work tirelessly to achieve their goals, and get nowhere, whilst others seem to effortlessly attract the things they want to themselves without missing breakfast, sleep or time spent in leisure, prayer or with family.

Regardless of how much effort, energy and money you pour into your work, your effort will not produce an abundant return if your modus operandi is not fundamentally principle-centred and consistent with the laws of life. It is not just effort that produces results - you have to have something that has the potential to work, otherwise you will be wasting precious time and energy trying to manifest something that cannot be manifested. '*Some things will not work because they do not work!*' What you are building will not stand, regardless of how closely you follow *your* pattern, if the pattern is not based on design and engineering principles. Without compliance to the laws of physics and mathematics buildings topple!

Because success leaves clues and laws work for anyone who makes use of them, a good work can be duplicated. A good work will be one that is based on principles from the Scriptures. Each of the laws mentioned in this study has a firm footing in the Judeo- Christian Scriptures. *This is why at Olive Branch we study, practice and teach evidence-supported, biblical values and principles for success and well-being.* As we work towards manifesting our finest and best we must endeavour to consistently build by what works — with patience, enthusiasm and determination — learning and applying ourselves to knowledge as we build. By seeking first the best and right ways of doing things, the things we desire often find their own way to us.

In your note book, make a list of what has worked for you and what hasn't, in the following areas of your life, where applicable: devotion to God, personal finance, relationships, realising a vision, choosing a career, physical and mental health, succeeding in business/ministry, growing a church, family life, raising children.

Success Modelling

"There are some things you don't have to know how it works. The main thing is that it works. While some people are studying the roots, others are picking the fruit. It just depends which end of this you want to get in on." Jim Rohn.

Day 42

Sabbath Week 6

Before I invite you to make your personal confessions of faith and to decide on this weeks' corresponding action, I want to summarise for you what we have discovered to date and how we might put them to work.

 God builds by design and works all things both natural and spiritual in the earth according to His predetermined plan, a plan based on the foreknowledge, wisdom and goodness of God. Building by design is what God intended for the human being in the earth. His will was that the human being would cause the will of God to be done on earth as it is being done in heaven. (Day 36)

- Not only does God build by design, His work of creation was progressively rolled out day by day over a period of a week. Rather than carry out separate individual acts, unrelated to anything before or after, God worked systematically and intelligently when creating the cosmos. His will continues to be carried out in the earth according to His action plan and timescale for the planet. (Day 37)

- According to the Creation narrative, God looked over the results of His activity and concluded that it was *'good'*. (Day 38) It was good because it looked everything like how He wanted it to look.

- Everything that God does proceeds from the perfections of His Personal Being and resembles Him in varying degrees of glory. We human beings are the masterpiece of Creation and are like God in the sense that He is our Creator and as our Creator we would naturally have features, characteristics and qualities that are from Him. The same can be said of the heavens and the earth; they too reflect the Person of God. (Day 39) They speak of God because

146

God invested Himself fully and personally in His work (day 40) and works all things in the earth according to the laws of life (Day 41)

 We manifest our finest and best work by building by the laws of life, biblical principles of how life works best. Our building plans should be based on these principles so that as we build by design the intelligence in the blueprint can be reflected in the work we are erecting.

- We should build according to what we have purposed and should build by the law of process, gradually and deliberately, on the back of a successful work. As we build by design we should be careful to regularly review our work so that what emerges reflects the person we are at the time we are building. As we give ourselves to the work it will take on the quality of our personal investment and will either be enthused with or starved of life.

Because I am committed to manifesting my finest and best work I will build by the laws of life, biblical principles of how life works best. I will apply myself to these principles so that as I build, the wisdom and intelligence in God's Word can be reflected in the work I am erecting.

I will build according to what I have purposed and will build patiently and incrementally until the work reaches its desired height. I give myself enthusiastically to the work and invest the best energies of my life towards making it a physical reality.

I will regularly review the work of my hands so that I build straight and true. I will welcome honest feedback, for faithful are the wounds of a friend.

 To take further the ideas of week 6, I will:

WEEK 7

Week 7
Day 43 - Speaking Well

 An important key to delivering our destiny is the use we make of words to shape our inner and outer realities. The Scriptures reveal that God remains passionate about and continues to speak well about His vision of the future. Regardless of the condition of the world He keeps on saying, *"as long as I live the whole earth will be full of my glory."* Regardless of the inconsistencies in the church He keeps on saying, *"I will have a glorious church."* God's confident words are not a denial of the present reality, rather they are statements based on His knowledge of the end from the beginning. When He speaks He is not hoping that it might be according to His word; He speaks because He has the final say in the future of the planet. When God speaks He looks beyond the present challenges to see the glorious future that He knows will have a physical, eschatological reality. When He speaks the external world aligns itself to His eternal Word. This is how He manifested the heavens and the earth. *(Genesis 1)* It was out of the abundance of His heart that He spoke His inner reality into existence.

 What you say to and about yourself, and to and about what you are working on will have a determining influence. Not only do the words we speak have an influence on us, they also effect our immediate environment. According to the Scriptures, inherent in the words we speak, are the powers of life and death - a power that includes the emotional potency of words to influence our inner lives.

"Words can cause us to erupt into laughter, break down into tears, fly into a rage, sink into despair, or float on clouds of happiness... the words we use do more than describe the events we experience and the actions we take;

> *they determine their outcomes. What I am today is the*
> *result of the words I have used. What I will become and*
> *experience tomorrow, depends on the words I use today."*
> *(Chuck Gallozzi)*

Because of the inherent power of words, it is important that the words of your mouth match the good vision in your eyes. What you believe and say most often ought to be a description of what you want to see, ideally, not necessarily what you are seeing, presently. The words of your mouth are very important to your success, particularly when what you are building is a great work or is experiencing difficulty. When the going gets tough and the vision in your eyes is proving elusive and troublesome, you must endeavour to continue to speak well of yourself, of others and about the present circumstances of your life. This advice is offered because it is very easy when feeling discouraged to use words to talk yourself out of your vision and to reduce your level of interest, motivation, faith and your level of physical and mental energy. Negative words spoken out of a depressed spirit will also discourage the energies of those around you and will lower their expectations and determination.

Speaking ill of what you are trying to achieve is also unhelpful because it changes your perception of the thing. Consequently, in addition to thinking and saying that *you* have not got what it takes, you are also saying that *the thing* is impossible to achieve. Very soon you lose the desire for the thing and the self-belief that it can be achieved.

When confidence and desire is lost, our words reflect this fact and lose their colour, fervour and energy. Unchecked we find ourselves in a spiralling negative lifestyle that was created by our own words. What happens illustrates *the law of expectation* - we all get what we confidently expect. Not what we would like, not even what we need, but what we confidently expect. What we confidently expect we tend to speak about and display in our behaviour and attitude.

Negative words are the voice of negative thoughts and negative thoughts are the products of negative imaginings. Negative imaginings arise when we focus on the challenges in the opportunity rather than on the opportunities in the challenge. To change a negative mindset we need to work on **how** we see. The realities of the external world - what can be seen - will not change until we change the way we see it and speak about it. To exercise the power of life inherent in healthy words we also need to change our vocabulary and support our new vocabulary with emotions and physical actions. One way to do this is through affirmations. Affirmations help the mind to give attention to what we value and believe about our life and the circumstances of our life. Affirmations are positive expressions of intent, desires, expectations, beliefs and values; principle-centred words of faith that describe the reality that we expect to see, rather than sentences that describe what we would like.

God's Word is powerful and effective because it comes out of the strength of His self-knowledge. Similarly, the words we speak as we build will come out of the strength of our beliefs about our first and second birth potential and will strengthen those beliefs. When we build according to these beliefs we experience success, which further strengthens our ability to be effective. This process is set in motion when we work on **how** we see and speak words that release life and not death. What better words to speak that what is true. Because God's Word is Truth, speaking His Word with the conviction and enthusiasm of faith will change your personal world.

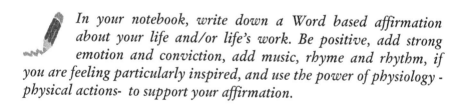

In your notebook, write down a Word based affirmation about your life and/or life's work. Be positive, add strong emotion and conviction, add music, rhyme and rhythm, if you are feeling particularly inspired, and use the power of physiology - physical actions- to support your affirmation.

Affirmations

"My thoughts have no substance until they are shaped into words. Once they become words they can be strung together to make statements. And the statements I make create my reality." *Chuck Gallozzi.*

Week 7
Day 44. - Delegation And Partnership

Even thought God is all powerful and knows all things, He delegates His creative activity in the earth to the human being and accomplishes much of His will in the earth through partners, people who freely and willing choose to work with Him. We see in the Genesis account that God delegated to Adam key features of His work of creation in the earth. (What Adam was given to do was no small undertaking; rather it was something that God Himself does - invest life). We also see that delegating key aspects of the work was what God had in mind from the beginning for the human being. It was not an after thought nor was it an attempt on the part of God to pass the problem of sin on to another to deal with. God knew from the beginning that He would need to prepare and make fit for purpose the human being for what He had imagined for Him in the earth. We also see in the Genesis account that God modelled for Adam how to act as a co-creator with Him in the earth *(Genesis 2:19-20)*, empowered Him to act in the earth, set the boundaries and scope of his authority, gave him a clearly defined area of responsibility and core tasks to undertake for which he would be responsible and held accountable. *(Genesis 1:28)*

We also see in the Genesis account, God releasing the human being's creativity by giving Adam more liberties than restrictions and how God makes Himself regularly available for fellowship and consultation with Adam, so that Adam would know the Person of God and not just know God as Lord and Master. Furthermore, we see in the Genesis account, throughout the Scriptures and in life, that God does not busy Himself in the affairs of the earth- He has put the human being in charge. We also see in the Genesis account that God created a complementary person to work alongside Adam, a person that would complement and support him in skills, attitudes, awareness, temperament, perspective, abilities. What we have in Genesis is a significant degree of trust and entrusting, which gives us a measure of the power and authority that God invested in the human being. We see in Jesus the same regard for the principles of delegation: He chose 12 apostles early in His ministry, made them fit for purpose—through modelling, teaching, working alongside them, shadowing and delegation— breathed into them and gave them authority to act and speak in His name.

 To manifest our finest and best work, we need to become masters in the art of reproducing ourselves in others (Day 39) and at empowering them to act and to speak in our name. If what you are working on is bigger than you, and it should be, you will need to have others working alongside you to help you with it. Even when you invest yourself in your work, (Day 40) your personal resources and investment will not be sufficient to manifest your finest and best work. A truly great work will be a collaborative work. (Day 23) We all need people to work the plan with us, and not just anybody. The people we bring alongside need to be in accord with us around the essentials of the vision (Day 26). Ideally, these people will be people that we have deliberately helped to fashion, people that we have prepared and made fit for purpose, people in whom we have personally breathed our lives into and influenced by example and exhortation (Days 39 & 40)

One of the major misunderstandings of delegation is that leaders should delegate to others menial tasks or tasks that they would rather not do. This practice suggests lack of trust in the delegate, insufficient knowledge of them and insecurity in the one doing the delegating. As we saw in the Genesis narrative, God gave to Adam tasks that He Himself would do, because He knew what He had fashioned the human being to accomplish. We also see in the Genesis account God releasing the human being's creativity by giving Adam more liberties than restrictions. This is important if you are going to draw out the qualities of your delegates. Tying their hands with 'red tape,' a plethora of rules and regulations and protocol arrangements will bind creativity. Similarly, standing over them and monitoring their every move will undermine their confidence. Notwithstanding, we also need people we can trust and entrust with authority and responsibility. This is why it is right to 'prove' people with regards to how well they exercise authority and handle responsibility and to increase what we entrust commensurate with their trustworthiness. To effectively manage this tension, the people we delegate responsibility to should have clearly defined areas of responsibility and accountability, core tasks to undertake and clear and explicit instructions about the extent of their authority.

We also need partners to work with and 'alongside.' These people, at best, will be equals - associates with whom we have a functional relationship and between whom there is mutual submission and support. (Day 23) These people will have complementary skills, attitudes, styles, temperaments, perspectives and abilities. They may even be people who came out from us, who now have their own identity, joined to us but not wholly dependent on us. *(Genesis 2:21-23)* This kind of relationship is valuable because partnership brings to bear on a situation the hearts and minds and personal resources of people who are committed to the same purposes and in covenant with each other. It provides companionship and friendship and builds up the trust that precedes entrusting.

In your notebook, write down the strengths and weaknesses of how you delegate authority; how you handle legitimate authority and how you work with partners.

Legitimate authority

"Manage by objectives. Tell people exactly what you want them to do and then get out of their way." Brian Tracy.

157

Week 7
Day 45 - Core Values And Core Business

When God created Adam He gave Him just a few core tasks: *'Be fruitful, multiply, exercise godly authority in the earth'* *(Genesis 1:28)* and a few core values to work His life around: *'follow through on the words of your Creator '* *(Genesis 2:16-17)*. In delegating authority to Adam, God was essentially saying to Adam, *"you are my co-creator in the earth and as my co-creator in the earth I want you to use the powers I put in you to do what I have asked of you."* Had Adam communicated the commission of the Creator to his wife and had they filled their days doing these few things, they would not have had time to entertain a stray thought in an idle moment. *(Genesis 3:6)* Experience teaches that when men sleep, are absent from the field of battle and are off task, the enemy comes in and sows ideas and thoughts that undermine the momentum that was there to be had from a job done well. *(Matthew 13:25)* Jesus got it right when He said, *"I must be about my Father's business."* *(Luke 2:45 NIV)* He knew what He had to do and did it consistently. He organised His entire life around the Father's priorities. Not a moment of His life was wasted.

Core business is about doing what must be done and doing it consistently well. It is about doing well the few things that make the most difference, the things that matter most, the things that are required to manifest your finest and best work. For example, if people are your business, you should not be spending only 20% of your time with them. If family is what matters most to you, why spend 80% of your time away from them? Rather than major on minor things, core business is about doing the things that produce the most effective outcomes for your life, family, church, ministry, business. By doing these things you will save yourself from being busy but ineffective. Many people have filled their lives with things, things that matter little and things that matter much.

The things that matter little take up much time and energy and produce very few tasteful fruit. The things that matter much are forced to the peripheries of life by what is often labelled extremely urgent and pressing.

So how might a person decide what things to make their core business? What should people be doing with the rest of their lives? How are we to decide between two or more good things, which one do we give priority? These issues of life and time management are important issues to address if we are to experience the fullness of our lives here on planet earth. Too many of us major on minor things, things that do not matter in the grand scheme of things. We get bogged down with trivia and invest our energies and resources of time, mind, will and affection in minor things. Although busy and active we often find ourselves falling short of our finest and best effort because we are unable or find it difficult to distinguish between important and urgent. Often we have selfish goals that serve only *'us four and no more.'* We are too busy with ourselves and our lives to think about anyone or anything else. What is lacking in these situations is a clear sense of Kingdom priorities. By Kingdom priorities I am referring to the most efficient and effective way to order and organise one's life and life's work on planet earth. Kingdom priorities are about the values, purposes, plans, pursuits and goals that have at their core the big picture (Day 54).

Kingdom priorities are things of eternal value; achievements that outlast your life, values that make your brief sojourn on the planet worthwhile, activities that contribute to the greater good. For the believer these priorities are: 1. Your relationship with God; 2. Your emotional, mental and physical health, 3. Your relationship with your family; 4. Your unique contribution towards the purposes of God for the planet; 5. Your work. 6. Your civil responsibilities as a citizen of your country. Your relationship with God is paramount because it informs and influences every area of your life and your emotional, mental and physical health is important because they are the states of being that enable you to contribute effectively to the other important areas of your life. Family is also important because they are the people over whom you have the greatest influence for good.

To live a life that is consistent with Kingdom priorities, we have to make good use of the time of our lives. Distracting peripherals that take our mind of task are to be avoided. We have to be deliberate when making decisions about priorities; we have to be wary of structures, policies, procedures, meetings and relationships that do not help, but hinder, the work of our hand. We also have to keep our lives free from the deception of being busy. Whilst multi-tasking can be a time efficient way to carry out our core business, multi-tasking is only efficient and effective if each task is begun, carried through effectively and completed on time. Similarly, if you are in a position to delegate core business to others, it is important that you do not have your people running around chasing their tails. If your people are too busy to pray, to think, to plan, to effectively do and to evaluate afterwards, they are not being as effective as they might be. It is better if you have them concentrate on the few things that make 80% of the difference rather than the many things that produce nothing more than 20% of the outcomes you want.

Once you know what you are about, the thing that will take you there is your sense of mission or vocation. By mission I mean what you do purposefully and deliberately on a daily basis because of what you want your life to accomplish. We are talking here about relevant and consistent actions that move you towards where you are heading. A person with a strong sense of mission knows what they need to do and does it. Core business is about doing and doing well what is required to fulfil the potential of our lives on the planet.

In your notebook, identify what and whose priorities you have ordered and organised your life around. What are you busy doing? Is your doing effective?

Kingdom Priorities

"Remember that you are needed. There is at least one important work to be done that will not be done unless you do it." Charles L. Allen (1848-99)

Week 7
Day 46 - Growth Potential

 God placed Adam and Eve in the Garden of Eden and commanded them to *"**Be fruitful, to multiply and to exercise godly authority in the earth'** (Genesis 1:28).* This command extended beyond the two of them and would involve them in making the whole earth like the Garden of Eden. It would mean taking the seeds of the Garden of Eden to the rest of the earth so that the whole earth could be filled with the bounties of the garden. Theirs would not be a mind numbing existence of maintenance only; God had more in mind for Adam than dressing the garden. *(Genesis 2:15)* The first commission, as stated, involved the whole earth coming under the influence and authority of a good God. What God had in mind for Adam and Eve was more than a good life for two - He had in mind a super abundant life for every living thing in the cosmos. As God's co-creator in the earth, Adam had boundless opportunity to extend the rule of God in the earth. God had given to him an open door, a significant piece of land to explore, subdue and make wonderful.

As the dominant species on the planet, human beings have been given divine licence to exercise our God-given ability and authority to affect and transform our environment - to create our own reality. God's will is that every human being makes good use of what He has placed within them, draws out the potential of God in each other and makes use of the good things that are in the earth. How we handle this responsibility and exercise this authority is our choice. As Adam was to find out to his and our detriment, this is best done in submission to the Kingdom of God. As people submitted to the authority of God and to Kingdom priorities, it's the church's privilege and responsibility to extend the Kingdom of God in the earth, to do our very best to fill the earth with the goodness of God.

What God has put in you and wants to bring into the earth through you is much bigger than you. It has to be, if you and what you carry are born of God. Every dream born of God is bigger than the dreamer— it goes beyond them and places a demand on them to stretch! The dream in your heart, the idea in your head, has to be more than what you can comfortably handle. It ought to be the sort of idea that you have to bring others alongside to help you with. It cannot just be about you and yours, *"us four and no more."* The cause you are engaged in will not be over until all families of the earth are blessed. Outside of your Eden, your garden paradise, your comfort zone, is a world waiting for you to effect. The good things that you have going on in your life and work has to flow out to areas where there is need. If it does not you will cease to grow and what you have going for you will stagnate. Your garden paradise, your wealthy place, your delightful land will be one of the snares of your success if you are content to bask in the sun and eat the fruits of your labour all day (Day 48).

Unlike your soul, that faints and grows weary and likes to take long comfort breaks, the human spirit wants to realise everything God placed within it. It wants to explore new things, plumb hidden depths, scale new heights, chart a way through the sea, and explore the universe. As this requires the cooperation of the soul, it is important that you do not let your mind, will and emotions frustrate the stirrings of your spirit.

Because exploring new things, plumbing hidden depths, scaling new heights, charting a way through the sea, exploring the universe, requires work, some have become content with what they have achieved and have settled. Even though there remains much unrealised potential within them and much ground to cover, they have yielded to the whims and moods of the soul and have become indifferent to the stirrings in their spirit. As a result they have lost the edge they once had. We see this in churches that have had tremendous numerical growth but no geographical or spiritual growth, the sort of growth that breaks new ground and takes new territory for the kingdom of God.

To keep the fires of godly ambition burning in your spirit (Day 5), the sort of fire that starts something new, overcomes self-imposed limitations by going beyond what has been before, it is important that you constantly feed your spirit with words of faith and testimonies of faith at work. Sadly, desire for more has fallen asleep in the lives of too many believers and needs to be aroused. Sometimes it takes a loud, annoying external stimuli to awaken dormant potential. Rather than having to be forcefully aroused out of needless slumber, it is better to be attentive to ones internal clock which says it is time to awake from sleep, it is time to arise and to build.

Because God has placed so much in you and within your reach, I must challenge you to become more by going for more. Do not settle for what has been accomplished, but rather press towards what your spirit has imagined. There is more land to be taken, more people to influence, more growth to be had, more potential to be tapped. There is room in the earth for more good. There is room in your life, church, ministry, enterprise, business, and venture for more growth, if you want it. Why not make a decision today to die empty.

> *"The secret to dying empty is living life to the full, giving it all your might and all you have got. Doing it until there is nothing left to do because you have become all you were created to be, done all you were designed to do and given all you were sent to give. Be satisfied with nothing less than your best." (Dr Miles Munroe, 1996)*

 In your notebook, briefly summarise the major achievements of your life and make a list of the things that you still want to accomplish. How ambitious are your future goals? What are they?

 Abundance Mentality

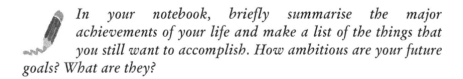 *"We must always change, renew, rejuvenate ourselves; otherwise we harden." Johann Wolfgang von Goethe (1749-1832).*

Week 7
Day 47 - Multiple Streams Of Supply

 The Garden of Eden was not only a beautiful and lush garden paradise because God planted it, *(Genesis 2:8)* and put the tree of life within it *(Genesis 2:9)* it also benefited from an internal spring that watered the ground *(Genesis 2:6)* the presence of God *(Genesis 3:8)* and a river that branched into four streams. Theses four streams contributed to the pleasantness and the fruitfulness of the garden. *(Genesis 2:10-14)* What we have in essence is a piece of land that has multiple streams of supply coming to it. Firstly, it is deliberately fashioned to be a wealthy place by the Creator. Secondly, centrally placed within it, is a life source that keeps it refreshed. Thirdly, it receives regular visits from One who is the wellspring of life and creativity. Fourthly, from within, it benefits from regular times of refreshing and fifthly, it is constantly refreshed by four streams that flow into it, around it and from it.

 Whatever you are working on will greatly benefit from being attached to multiple streams of supply. To survive and thrive your life and life's work, family, church, ministry, venture, enterprise, business, needs to be constantly invigorated and refreshed by five sources of supply. Firstly, each area of your life has to be deliberately fashioned and set up to be a wealthy place by hands that have unreservedly embrace the abundance mentality. If you want your life and life's work, family, church, ministry, venture, enterprise, business, to be abundant, healthy, expanding and blessed, you have to make it that way. It will not happen if your soul is resistant to the stirrings of your spirit to go after something large, exciting and grand. (Day 45) A wealthy place is the work of a wealthy mind, the product of large thinking, in the same way that small thinking produces impoverished lifestyles. Remember, we all create in our image and produce after our kind. (Day 39) This is why it is important that you personally benefit from these multiple streams of supply. Without them you die! If you die, so will your work for you are the one that gives it life.

Secondly, the values of life, growth, learning, change and potential has to be a central feature of your life and life's work. If they are, these values will flow through the whole of your operation and will affect everything you do. If they are not placed centrally, your life and life's work will become staid, cold and harsh and sin and death will rule. When this happens the whole thing becomes hard and onerous and the things that you did not want in your life will spring up and take root. By eating regularly from the tree of life, the Lord Jesus Christ, we allow ourselves to partake of the fruits of His life, namely life, growth, learning, change and the release of our potential. To keep ourselves and our life's work continuously refreshed it is also important that we isolate, point out to others and avoid things that stifle and choke the good things that are ours to enjoy. (Day 48).

Thirdly, for our life and life's work to be further refreshed it is also important that we meet regularly with people whose presence, knowledge and manner of life leaves us inspired, refreshed, challenged and invigorated. It is good to have these people as friends, people with whom we can walk with *'in the cool of the day.' (Genesis 3:8)* Even when these people are outside of our life's work, family, church, ministry, venture, enterprise, business, it works to our advantage to regularly welcome their input.

Fourthly, for our life and life's work to be a perpetual flow of life, it is important that we are able to nourish ourselves and be self-sustaining. In the same way that the Garden of Eden benefited from regular times of refreshing from within *(Genesis 2:6),* we need to be able to refresh ourselves. As individuals we must take responsibility for keeping ourselves refreshed and energised, spiritually, emotionally, intellectually, socially and physically. Similarly, in family and church life, as in ministry and business, we need to give regular time to sharing, caring, listening to and being with each other. When this happens, alongside individuals nourishing their own lives, each person brings into their meetings with others their personal energy. As a result, what they achieve together is far greater than what they experienced on their own.

Fifthly, for our life and life's work, family, church, ministry, venture, enterprise, business, to realise their growth potential, they must have constantly flowing into them streams of new information, resources, ideas, creativity. These things nourish it from within. They also need ways of directing that flow outwards to untouched/parched areas around it so that others might benefit. These untouched areas will place a demand on their potential and will release it. If the flow is inwards only the whole thing will stagnate. As human beings, we need to express ourselves externally or we become staid and the growth potential within our work becomes frustrated. By availing yourself of various sources of life, you help yourself maintain the freshness, the vitality, the enthusiasm needed to make every venture that you are involved with bountiful.

In your notebook, identify the sources of supply that you have coming into your life/life's work. By this I mean the things, the resources, the people, and the places that nourish you spiritually, emotionally, intellectually, socially, physically and financially.

Sabbath Principle

"Employ your time in improving yourself by other men's writings, so that you shall gain easily what others have laboured hard for." Socrates. *"We must learn to apply all that we know so that we can attract all that we want."* Jim Rohn.

Week 7
Day 48 - Threats from Within

The fact that Adam and Eve sinned in their garden paradise should be a sobering thought, especially for those who feel that their great success inoculates them from failure. Though Adam and Eve had so much going for them and were created flawless, they used free will to act on a desire that they did not know they had, a desire that laid dormant within them until stroked. A close look at the Genesis account reveals internal threats to success that have to be isolated and resisted. We hinted at these threats on Day 44 when we said, *"Had Adam communicated the commission of the Creator to his partner and had they filled their days doing these few things, they would not have had time to entertain a stray thought in an idle moment. **(Genesis 3:6).**

In the Genesis narrative we see ***ignorance and idleness*** at work. Ignorance and idleness are two of the most deadly threats to success that have to be guarded against. Experience teaches that ignorance is not bliss, that what you don't know will hurt you and that the devil makes work for idle hands and minds.

On Day 45 we made passing reference to another threat when we said that, your garden paradise, your wealthy place, your delightful land will be one of the snares of your success if you are content to bask in the sun and eat the fruits of your labour all day. Thus, the third threat to continued success is *self -satisfaction*. *"**The greatest threat to being all you could be is satisfaction with who you are. What you could do is always endangered by what you have done."** (Dr Miles Munroe)* The threats to success that Adam and Eve had to contend with are referred to in the Bible as the lusts of the flesh, the desire of the eyes and the pride of life *(1 John 2:16)*. Every human being has these threats from within to contend with. According to Matthew 4, Jesus was similarly challenged. However, unlike Adam, He resisted these threats from within, choosing rather to remember what was written (Day 30) and what His life was about. (Day 45)

 One of the benefits of formative evaluations we identified on Day 38 is that interim checks keep our lives free from unhelpful baggage that unwittingly undermine our work. Interim internal checks keep us in touch with ourselves— the inner workings of our soul - our attitudes, thoughts, values, motives and behaviours. Within each of us there are dangers to our success that have to be isolated and resisted. Every one of us has things about us that if left unchecked or if we are ignorant about can cause us to self-sabotage. Not to think so is naïve. History is replete with examples of people who had so much going for them, but tore it all down because they did not give heed to changes within them that indicated a fundamental shift in attitude, thinking, values and motive. As a result they had to leave it all behind because they got involved in an improper sexual relationship; had severe problems with alcohol and low self esteem; had problems managing other people's finance; were prone to outbursts of anger and aggression, severe mood swings and depression; had difficulty managing their home life; had problems in speaking the truth and with being challenged.

Because matters of the heart can seriously and significantly undermine our work, we will isolate these threats to success with reference to Adam.

The concern off being off task is a serious one. It is in such moments, when our hands and mind are not engaged in relevant activity, that our hearts can be distracted by the pull of trivial pursuits. For this reason we must ensure that our waking moments are spent with people doing those things that relate to our core business. *Self-seeking*, is another threat. This is where our interests, desires, ambitions, wants, feelings, preferences and wishes become central in our thought life and in decision making. Adam and Eve's enticement to sin happened because they put their interests, desires, ambitions, wants, feelings, preferences and wishes above God's revealed will. They entertained a view of themselves that caused them to act unilaterally and in their own interests. In placing themselves centrally they made subservient what was meant to occupy primary place. Adam and Eve saw themselves as being central to the operation and entertained thoughts of *self-aggrandisement.*

The offer from the adversary was an offer that promised increased knowledge, power, status and influence. It was an incitement to get involved in a power struggle, to topple the regime, with a view to them becoming Chief Officer. When Adam and Eve ate of the tree of the knowledge of good and evil, they acted independently of God, the Chief Officer. They disregarded the principle of accountability because they thought that their self–willed actions would serve them better than having to work under the covering of authority. They sought to be self-made individuals and by acting in this way displayed their pride and arrogance. A fall was inevitable!

Adam and Eve had no justifiable reason to feel insecure, to feel that they were being denied a great opportunity for promotion—they had been given everything! God's benevolence and goodness had given them a significant place to occupy in the earth and had given them an abundance of wealth to enjoy. They enjoyed rich fellowship with God, with others in the earth, and with the earth itself. They lacked for nothing in all the dimensions of life— spiritual, physical, emotional, social, moral, psychological, intellectual, environmental and cosmological. Why they acted in the manner that they did cannot be put down solely to innocence or ignorance. They knew God and knew what was right! Theirs was a voluntary and deliberate act to do differently to what they knew to be right. What they reaped in their lives is a poignant reminder to us to be wilful and deliberate in doing well what we know is right, even when the desires within and the opportunities from without to do behave differently are compelling.

 In your notebook, make a list of the unhelpful habits, behaviours, attitudes, thoughts and beliefs that have become a regular part of your life. How might you live free of their negative influence?

 Self-Sabotage - Achievement with Virtue

"I count him braver who overcomes his desires than him who

169

conquers his enemies, for the hardest victory is over self." *Aristotle (384-322 BC)* "There are no finer sensations in life that which comes with victory over one's self... Go forward to a goal of inward achievement, brushing aside all your old internal enemies as you advance." *Vash Young*

Day 49
Sabbath Week 7

Before I invite you to make your personal confessions of faith and to decide on this weeks' corresponding action, I want to summarise for you what we have discovered to date and how we might put them to work.

 God remains passionate about and continues to speak well of His vision of the future. Regardless of the condition of the world He keeps on saying, *"as long as I live the whole earth will be full of my goodness."* Regardless of the inconsistencies in the church, He keeps on saying, *"I will have a glorious church."* God looks beyond the present challenges to the see the glorious future that He said and keeps saying will come into being. When He speaks the external world aligns itself to His eternal Word. (Day 43)

 Even thought the Almighty Creator is all-powerful and knows all things, He delegated His creative activity in the earth to the human being and accomplishes much of His will in the earth through partners, people who freely chose to work with Him. (Day 44) God delegated to Adam just a few core tasks: *'Be fruitful, multiply, exercise godly authority in the earth.'*

- In delegating authority to Adam, God was essentially saying to Adam, *"you are my co-creator in the earth and as my co-creator in the earth I want you to use the powers I put in you to do what I have asked of you."* (Day 45) This mandate stretched beyond just the two of them and would involve making the whole earth like the Garden of Eden. It would mean taking the seeds within the garden to the rest of the earth so that the whole earth could be filled with the bounties of the garden. (Day 46) Contributing to the bounties of the garden were multiple streams of

ion*

supply that flowed within it and through it. (Day 47) Unfortunately, all this was to come to a gradual end because of an act of their will that compromised the life source of the garden. (Day 48)

- The words we speak over our life and life's work carry tremendous power. Not only do the words we speak have an influence on us and those who hear us, they also effect our immediate environment. Inherent in the words we speak are the powers of life and death.

- Because a truly great work will be a collaborative work, we need to have alongside us people who can be trusted and entrusted with responsibility - people who know what they need to do, give it priority and follow through. The work we are engaged in also needs to have sufficient growth potential to keep ourselves and others occupied for a lifetime. It needs to be regularly enthused with life and those involved with it need to keep themselves free from destructive issues of the heart.

Because I am committed to manifesting my finest and best work, I will speak well over my life and life's work and will be careful to speak words that bring life and not death. I will speak well of the people I work with and will uphold and encourage them with my words, actions and attitude.

I will support and empower those I have entrusted with responsibility and where I am entrusted with authority will show myself to be faithful and accountable. I will work collaboratively with the partners I am in covenant with and will seek to give them the advantage. I commit myself to the core tasks of my vision and refuse to be sidetracked.

I resist complacency and self-satisfaction and stir myself up to go after more, until I have fully discharged my mandate to increase, extend, grow and expand as a human being. I make every effort to keep my spirit, soul and body and the work of my hand refreshed, enthused and

172

invigorated and resist the threats to success that lie within. I submit myself to people and systems that will help me to achieve my vision with virtue.

 To take further the ideas of week 7, I will:

WEEK 8

Week 8
Day 50 - Threats From Without

Not only must we be aware of threats from within that if left unchecked can cause us to self-sabotage, we must also safeguard our work from threats from without. Genesis 3 is an account of an external threat that Adam and Eve failed to deal with. A threat from without that brought about the fall of humanity. What we have in the account is the approach of an enemy whose aim was to bring to an end the good things that Adam and Eve had going on in their lives and in their environment. From what we know of this enemy he should have been strongly and forcefully resisted. According to the Bible this particular enemy of humanity once had a successful place in life but compromised his lofty position and success when he acted on his desire for self-aggrandisement. Like Adam and Eve he was a righteous, holy and rational being that could chose how to act. Like Adam and Eve he occupied a prime place in his sphere of influence. Like Adam and Eve he served faithfully in his area of service, until he acted on a desire to go against the natural order of things. (Day 48) Unrepentant, his nature became corrupt and he became envious of the success that others enjoyed.

The Bible refers to this fallen being as Satan and ascribes many titles to him to describe how he operates as an enemy from without. He is called the 'Liar' because He distorts and misrepresents God and the Truth of God. *(Genesis 3: 1:3; John 8:44)* He is called the 'Devil' because his character and ways are deceitful, devious, manipulative and cunning. *(Genesis 3:1,4)* He is called 'Belial', a term which represents him as a troublesome, mischievous scoundrel who likes to worm his way in and out of situations, leaving a trail of destruction behind him; a worthless, good for nothing that has fallen from his purpose in life. *(2 Corinthians 6:15)* He is called the 'Tempter' because He knows the crooked propensities and inclinations in fallen human nature and how to exploit them to his advantage. He works through the lusts of the flesh, the desires of the eyes and the pride of life (Day 48). His way is that of enticement. *(Genesis 3:6; 2 Corinthian 6:15)* His wish is to steal, kill and destroy godly achievement, forward movement and the extension of the Kingdom of God in the earth. *(John 10:10)* He is to be resisted by appealing to the values of your life and venture *(Matthew 4: 4)*

Your decision to fulfil your place in the big picture (Day 54) to go after a different life, your big idea, your grand vision of the future will provoke in those who are unhappy with their personal circumstances, criticism, envy, jealousy, fear, resentment, hostility, malicious and subversive actions, ill will, ill feeling, bitterness, slander, malice. Not to think so is dangerously naïve. It is a fact of life that some people will see the enthusiasm and light that you bring and the progress you are making as a threat to be extinguished. It would seem from their reactions that the light your carry provokes and exposes, by its very nature, the threats within them that have undermined their progress and forward movement. (Day 48) Rather than confess their faults and be helped and healed *(James 5:16)* they would rather tear down what you are faithfully building. Some feel that they must make the exposure of your weaknesses their vocation in life. Some even feel that they must save you from yourself. Such people are keen to find fault with your operations and feel that they owe it to others to warn them about you. What they fail to see are the weaknesses of character that have held them back.

What we are speaking of here is not healthy competition from without that provokes people to excellence, nor are we referring to the natural concern of friends and family for our daring and often risky venture of faith. We are talking about words and actions that are meant to upset, hurt and harm. Like the Devil, some of our enemies slither their way into our affairs and come across as friends, in an attempt to draw us away from our core business and to have us act in ways that are not in keeping with the values of our venture. The words they speak are to be resisted and they are to be the objects of prayer. Even though Jesus rebuked Peter for having thoughts and speaking words that were not in keeping with the values of His venture *(Mark 8:33)* He also prayed for him, for he saw behind his words and actions the enemy at work. *(Luke 22:31-32)*

To guard against such things it is important when sharing your aspirations and heart with people outside your let us team to exercise self-restraint. Many innovators can speak of the perils of sharing their ideas with people who promised to help them flesh it out, only to have the idea stripped of its essential components to the degree that the idea no longer look likes the image of its creator. What follows is disheartening. The idea is taken over and is fashioned by the head and heart of another. It now bares no resemblance to the person who conceived it and enthused over it from birth. Though they might still be involved with the idea, the idea develops in a different direction and takes on the values, ambitions and personality of its new owners. When this happens the conceiver of the idea has given birth to an idea that is being raised by someone else. Some how they need to find a way to redeem the idea so that they might once again own it and be in a position to raise and grow it in their own image.

To avoid this tricky situation it is better not to enter into it, but to conceive and raise the idea with partners who will support you in bringing the idea to maturity, rather than unknown individuals who are not in covenant with you. The best way to resist the threats from without is to keep a check on the threats from within (Day 48), to do what has been agreed (Day 26) and to keep the big picture foremost in your mind (Day 54). This way you do not give your enemies a foothold.

In your notebook, identify the main external threats to your venture and develop a strategy for resisting them.

Dream Thieves

"Envy is the mud, failures throw at success." Chuck Gallozzi.

Week 8
Day 51 - Seeing The Challenges Through

According to biblical history, over 6000 years have passed since God carried out His first action towards making His vision for the human being a reality. The Old Testament charts 4000 years of God's activity in the earth, prior to the coming of the Messiah, and the New Testament covers about 100 years of God's activity in the earth through the church. Even though many centuries have come and gone since the coming of the Messiah, God continues to work His predetermined plan in the earth. He has not lessened in His passion to see the whole earth filled with the knowledge of the glory of God. He remains committed to the vision that was determined at the counsel of the Godhead in eternity past. Even when He experienced early on feelings of sadness that He had entrusted a large part of His vision for humanity to the human being *(Genesis 6:6)* He has not ceased to work in and through and with the human being, He has stayed with the human being for His vision is about His glory in the species of being He created in His image.

Even though His vision of the future has been challenged by sin, selfishness, rebellion, atheistic belief systems, scandals and schisms in the church and ungodliness within the very people who would make His vision a reality, He is undeterred and undaunted. He has seen every challenge through and expects to see what He had in mind come into being. With long patience He has waited to see the manifestation of the sons of God coming into their destiny. His vision is fast becoming a reality in the earth.

A great house takes time to build, which is why seeing the challenges through is important if you are going to manifest your finest and best work. The beautiful cathedrals that occupy prime positions in our cities took 100s of years to complete. People have come and gone but they remain. The people who conceived the idea and who laid the first stone are gone and so are the people who invested their skills, resources and time in the building of it. These building have out lasted them all. They have survived threats from within (Day 48) and threats from without (Day 50); survived crises of financial and material resources and labour, changing political circumstances, natural disasters and deliberate acts of criminal damage. They remain because they were built to endure and were designed to facilitate a purpose that transcends their place in the earth. (Day 54)

Similarly, your life and life's work have not been without challenge. Like most people with an audacious vision, you too have had to deal with threats from within and from without. Only you and those close to you can speak of the internal struggles, the crises of confidence, the fears, the insecurities, the anxiety, the disappointments, frustrations and the doubts that you have experienced. The times you have cried, been unable to eat, sleep and think because of the enormity of the work and the shortage of personal finance, support, opportunity, mental and physical energy and emotional strength. Only you can speak of the times you came close to giving up, the number of times you had to find the courage to begin again and the knocks you have had to patiently endure.

Like every person on the road to manifestation, you can also speak about the personal growth challenges and the steep learning curves that you have had to embrace in order to keep progressing on the road to manifestation, and the public walk and talk you had to maintain so not to dishearten those who looked to your for their strength.

You may also know what it feels like to be misunderstood, misrepresented, judged, criticised and strongly opposed. Perhaps those you thought were friends have forsaken you in your hour of need. Perhaps you have seen people leave when they said that they would stay and people enthusiastically welcome you one moment only to request your crucifixion moments later. Maybe you have fallen in public only to discover that you have very few people willing to provide support. Or perhaps one in your company betrays you to those who seek your downfall. Maybe you know the experience of seeing the people around you capitulate in the face of challenge or the experience of having your reputation tarnished and your good misrepresented. These issues come to the best of us. What we make of these experiences and how we manage ourselves in these circumstances is crucial to our success. Each test, challenge, frustration can be shaped and used as a learning experience, an opportunity for personal growth and leadership development. By greeting the challenges this way we empower ourselves to see these challenges through and develop the strength of character required to manifest and administer a great work.

In your notebook, make a note of the major challenges of your life and life's work that you have seen through. What does this say about you and the vision in your eyes?

Resolve

"A leader, once convinced that a particular course of action is the right one, must be undaunted when the going gets tough."
Ronald Reagan

Week 8
Day 52 - Summative Evaluations

At the end of the 6th day, God assessed all that He had done and concluded that it was *"very good" (Genesis 1:31)*. He was able to come to this summative judgment because His formative evaluations (Day 38) had given Him interim measures of the likely end result of all His activity. Because all that God had determined at the planning phase of Creation had been achieved, there was no further need for Him to do any more. He could now cease from labour and enter into rest.

In the Christian faith the Judgement Seat of Christ is the place where each believer gets to hear God's summative evaluation of their work, before they enter His rest. *(2 Corinthians 5:10; Revelation 22:12).* According to the Scriptures faithfulness will be a key criterion in God's summing up of our work. *(1 Corinthians 4:2-5)* Thus, the Judgment Seat of Christ is an objective measure against explicit criteria. It will not be about whether we passed or failed the requirements for salvation but about the quality of our service. In order to hear the highest of commendation of all - *'Well done good and faithful servant,' (Matthew 25:23)* it should be the habit of every believer to regularly carry out formative evaluations of their life and life's work against the criteria of God's Word and to build by the Book (Day 36). It will be against the Book that our work will be measured.

Summative evaluations involve a thorough assessment of the end results of a job, project, piece of work, so that progress can be measured and a judgment about productivity announced and recorded. Even though summative evaluations take place at the end of a piece of work, they are intrinsically linked to their beginning, when SMART goals were determined. As we saw on Day 32, SMART stands for **S**pecific, **M**easurable, **A**ctivity, **R**elevant and **T**imescale. By specific we mean that the goal can be clearly stated — it is specific, definite, unambiguous and unequivocal, rather than a general statement of intention that is difficult to define and measure. The notion of being able to measure achievement of a goal is a valid one and speaks of being able to assess, gauge, and quantify the overall impact of relevant activity on an objective. Thus a key feature of summative evaluations is that they are based on immovable criteria - the success criteria we agreed when we developed our plan of action. Because each objective is written in a 'SMART way', there is no uncertainty about whether what we hoped to achieve has been accomplished. It will be obvious!

At best, summative evaluations will include a thorough examination of our work, so that we have a detailed understanding of *what* has been achieved, *how* it was achieved and *how well* it has been achieved. A good summative evaluation will give us more than quantitative data- whether we succeeded or failed - it would also provide us with qualitative information so that we can learn more about the achievement. There is little to be gained from knowing that a job was deemed good, unless we also know: *why* it was deemed good- because it fulfilled our success criteria- and in *what* ways it is good - because it was carried out faithfully. A good summative evaluation will also take into account the ongoing formative evaluations of our lives and life's work (Day 38) so that the whole picture can be considered when reaching a final judgment.

In this regard summative evaluations are similar to the practice of arriving at an overall and final grade about a student's work, based on the marks they got for the assignments they completed over the length of the course. This type of assessment not only measures the final outcome, it also measures application and effort over time.

It would be most unfortunate to come to the end of one's life, to finish a major undertaking, only to find that it was way off the mark. That feeling can be likened to the futile experience of writing reams for an examination question that was incorrectly understood. Though the student may have exerted much effort and given that question a lot of time, because the answer did not have the information that the examining body were looking for it would receive a low mark. In your life and life's work you want to be more than busy working, doing and living, you want to be on track. This is why it pays to be familiar with the criterion against which your life and life's work will be judged, to live and to work by this criterion and to regularly measure your life and work against them. In so doing you save yourself from the stress of an uncertain outcome.

 In your note book, give 10 examples from your own life/work of how you would want the following sentence to be completed: Well done good and faithful servant, you have (for example) shown yourself trustworthy in your handling of other people's money.

 Success Criteria

 "I don't want to get to the end of my life and find that I have just lived the length of it. I want to have lived the width of it as well." Diane Ackerman (b. 1948)

Week 8
Day 53 - Celebrating Success

We said yesterday that the Judgement Seat of Christ is the place where each believer gets to hear God's summative evaluation of what they did with the life and the gifts He gave to them. Because the Judgment Seat of Christ is about rewards for service, it will also be a time of rejoicing and celebration, a time where achievements are recognised, acknowledged and celebrated. According to the Scriptures, Christ will give believers crowns for showing faithfulness in their area of service. For example, those who faithfully endure temptation will receive a crown of life. *(James 1:12; Revelation 2:10)* Those who eagerly look forward to His return will receive a crown of righteousness *(2 Timothy 4:8)* and those who faithfully shepherd the flock of God will receive a crown of glory. *(1 Peter 5: 4)* The occasion will culminate with the joining of the church and the Christ at the Marriage of the Lamb. Every believer gets to participate in the Marriage Supper. This will be a time of great celebration for the people that God said that He would have in the beginning, have come into the fullness of the stature of Christ.

I can think of no better way to end the 'day' than with a celebration of achievement - the sort of inclusive celebration that leaves every member of the team with something to celebrate. Celebrating achievement involves reviewing the success criteria of our SMART action plan, so that we can see explicitly the link between the desired outcomes that we had in mind and what has actually been achieved (Day 32). It also involves revisiting our 5WH planning approach so that we can be specific in recognising achievement. The 5WH approach makes it possible for recognition to be specific, detailed and a true reflection of the involvement of each person in the success story of the team, rather than a casual well done to all (Day 31). Celebrating success also involves looking over our formative evaluations in order to get a measure of the distance travelled and the obstacles that have been overcome (Day 38). Thus, as well as being an opportunity to mid course correct, formative evaluations are also opportunities to celebrate success, so that even though there remains much to do, the good that has been done is recognised. Summative evaluations should also have this feature; for they represent the moment we make our closing statements about what has been achieved, before we finally sign off the work. Considered together, celebrating success is about acknowledging that ***together*** we have achieved ***what we set out to achieve*** because ***people worked at it, overcame obstacles and showed real commitment.***

Contrary to common practice, celebrating success does not necessarily have to come at the end of a long run, for example after 35 years in ministry or at the end of a person's life. It is better to recognise success on an ongoing basis than at the end of a great life or endeavour, when those who need to hear about it and learn from it are no longer with us. Celebrations are simply occasions that mark and recognise the successful completion of activity. In this context, celebrating success is more than an event or an occasion, but a habit that flows out of an attitude of gratitude. It is an attitude that shows appreciation in word and deed for what people have provided, given and done.

Another misunderstanding of celebrating success is that recognising achievement encourages people to slacken off and to become complacent. The thinking behind this view is that people are motivated primarily by external rewards and that once they have been rewarded they will have no reason to apply more effort. Whilst external rewards are important, because they provide extrinsic motivation, they are not the primary motivators of those who take seriously their personal development. Such people are not given to slacking off— they want to reach for more, if only to experience the internal rewards of achievement and accomplishment. Their primary motivation is not the obtaining of things from without but the realising of personal potential.

Another misunderstanding of celebrating success is that if the objectives we set ourselves have not been achieved, then what is required is not celebration but commiseration and a stern rebuke. Whilst it is important to acknowledge shortfalls, the morale that raises self-confidence and stimulates performance is boosted by recognition of the effort, energy and interest that was invested. In this way, its not just those who came first and who did the most who are recognised but everyone who played a part. Being generous with praise is important because praise confirms success, builds confidence and encourages more effort. It is a good thing to generously give to another as well as a good thing to receive. We all take kindly to being appreciated and we all like to receive as an exchange for our best efforts, some external recognition in kind, whether that is a gift, a team celebration, a day off, a night out, financial or material reward, a certificate, an award. As we all have people that we are working with and alongside, it is important that our words and actions encourage and support those around us (Day 43). The good they do is to be acknowledged and the environment in which they operate should be a learning culture that places their personal growth and well-being above the achievement of corporate goals. Whilst recognising success can take many forms, from a word of acknowledgement to a lavish formal occasion, it is important that celebrations are meaningful and commensurately recognise the effort and the gains being celebrated.

In your notebook, write down ways in which you could recognise achievement in yourself and in others. Now act on them!

Attitude of Gratitude

"The man is a success who has lived well, laughed often, and loved much; who has gained the respect of intelligent men and the love of children; who has filled his niche and accomplished his task; who leaves the world better than he found it, whether by an improved poppy, a perfect poem, or a rescued soul; who never lacked appreciation of earth's beauty or failed to express it; who looked for the best in others and gave the best he had." Proverbs 15:1 Bible (15th-16th centuries)

Week 8
Day 54 - The Big Picture

 The account of the Tower of Babel in Genesis 11 teaches that it is possible to achieve a significant measure of success by applying the *Principles of Creation* outlined in this book and still miss out on God's finest and best for your life. Genesis 11 is an example of how a group of people used the themes of this book to manifest their own physical reality. In the account we observe the following *Olive Themes:* personal responsibility, conceiving ideas, enthusiasm, commitment, faith, vision, visualisation, imagination, beginning, covenant, corresponding activity, SMART planning, building by design, building on the previous, personal investment, unity, partnership, growth potential.

So deliberate and effective was Nimrod and his team's application of these principles of creation, that the Godhead, *"came down to see the city and the tower that the men were building"* and remarked, *"if as one people speaking the same language they have begun to do this, then nothing that they have planned to do will be impossible to them. (Genesis 11:5-6 NIV)*

Their actions got the attention of the Godhead and received the highest commendation of faith– *"all things are possible to those who believe!" (Mark 9:23)* Unfortunately, the work of their hands missed a crucial principle of this book— *"Unless the LORD builds the house, its builders labour in vain" (Psalm 127:1 NIV).* Their work failed because it was tainted with the same attitudes of ignorance and self-aggrandisement that brought about the fall of Lucifer and of Adam and Eve. It came to nothing because God frustrates the efforts of those who are concerned with empire building. The account is a poignant reminder that our work will not succeed ultimately unless the glory goes to God. Those who seek glory: praise, recognition, honour, the esteem of the crowd, exaltation, must be careful that their work is not marred by their own dirty hands (Day 48). Those who wish to ascend the hill of the Lord must have clean hands and pure hearts. *(Psalm 24:3-4)*

 It is truly amazing what people can accomplish if they have a mind to work (Day 33). According to the Scriptures, human beings are like Elohim in that we are capable of creating our own physical reality. This is the gift of God to humanity (Day 1). What we do with our power and authority to create in the earth is the responsibility of each one of us. We could, for example, use our powers to great effect to serve a cause that contributes to the greatest good, the big picture, or we could use those same powers to design a life that makes us a name, but nothing more. Such a life is lived in the here and now, for the here and now, and does not extend into eternity. The big picture, on the other hand transcends this temporal plane. It goes beyond what we might want or wish for ourselves. It goes beyond our needs, desires, ambitions, aspirations and goals. It is essentially about the will of God being done in the earth through us! What makes life truly worthwhile is when we use our creative potential, our whole selves, in showing God's goodness to others.

Many people have used their human resources to erect great edifices that have served humanity and the Kingdom of God well. They are to be commended for sharing with us the gifts and goodness of the Creator towards our planet. Unfortunately, the vast majority of the people of the earth spend their lives and human resources pursuing things that do not connect them to the Creator or to the purpose that requires their place in the Cosmos. Many of them speak of feelings of insignificance, of purposelessness and of the emptiness of secular pursuits. What they long to experience is the joy of being part of something bigger than themselves, the thrill of experiencing the fullness of their lives and of fulfilling their destiny. What they lack is a compelling why, a why that has at is core the well being of others and the honour and glory of God (Day 11).

As co-creators in the earth, in covenant with God, Christian believers are on the planet to do something unique with their lives in their generation. We are here to do a work that transcends the temporal, something that is of earthly use but supremely of eternal significance. We are here to extend the kingdom of God in the earth so that the whole earth bares witness to the love of God towards the human being *(Numbers 14:12).* This is the vision that God had in mind for the human being in the beginning. A vision that is advanced as we actively and deliberately make His will, His word, His purposes, plans and priorities the core business of our brief sojourn on the planet (Day 45). To do a work in the earth that can be carried over into eternity, it is important that we organise our lives around the priorities of the Kingdom of God (Day 45)— things of eternal value, words and actions that leave the world better than how we found it, values that make our sojourn on the planet worthwhile, activities that contribute to the greater good.

There is no better way to spend the days of your life than in the service of your Creator. The things that you are working on and giving your best attention will receive a favourable summative evaluation from God at the Judgment Seat of Christ (Day 52) and will be a cause for celebration (Day 53) if it is based on the will and glory of God. Such things are built to last!

In your notebook, give examples of how you have made the Kingdom of God the priority of your life. What more could you do?

The Kingdom of God

"Keep your eye on eternal goals." John H. Groberg. "Have you had a kindness shown? Pass it on; 'twas not given for thee alone, Pass it on; Let it travel down the years, Let it wipe another's tears, Till in Heaven the deed appears, Pass it on." Henry Burton.

Week 8
Day 55 - Continuing Without You

Once God had carried out His summative evaluation of creation, on the 6th day, He ceased from all His work *(Genesis 2:2)*. He had finished what He set out to do and would now be standing in a different relationship to His work. He would no longer be directly involved but would be handing the rest of the work over to the person that He fashioned and breathed His life into - the human being (Day 40). Although the work would still speak of its Founder and His Spirit would continue to be present in the earth, the earth would now also reflect the quality of the being that God put in charge. It was now down to the human being to build according to God's design (Day 36) and to make the whole earth like the Kingdom of Heaven (Day 46). In handing the earth over to the human being to steward, God literally entrusted the human being with the responsibility and power to build on what He had started. By issuing this mandate to the human being, to be the ruling species on the planet, God defined the boundaries of His relationship with the earth and the human beings influence in the earth. Though still involved in the earth, God would have sovereign oversight of the operation and would intervene if His counsel was requested and if the request was in keeping with His covenant with humanity.

By delegating power and authority to the human being, God entrusted the human being with the good work that He had brought into being out of nothing (Day 17). It was His will that the whole thing would continue without His direct involvement and would not lose any of it essential characteristics. It took faith in His workmanship for God to put a large part of His vision into the hands of the human being. Even though He knew that the earth would take a different direction to the one He had in mind and felt sadness when the human being marred His work, because of the greatness of His investment in the human, He stayed with the being He had created in His image (Day1).

It takes a secure person to walk away from a wor. have invested heavily in and raised to greatness out of Not many people have this quality about them, to leave work behind in order to start again, out of nothing. All aro. us there are good people who have built a great work who are now sitting a the top of that work. They dare not release it to God in order to start another work. The reason why they hold on to what they have accomplished and acquired is because it is the thing that defines them— the thing that brought them fame and fortune, honour, prestige and influence. Such people think that building a great work makes them a great person. What they fail to realise is that a truly great work is one that can continue without them and a truly great person is one who is able to entrust the work to another in order to build again out of nothing, because the Master requires it. A work that still relies heavily on its founder is not a great work. Such a work will fold as soon as the founder is no longer around, because it was founded on them. In order for a work to be a great work it has to be able to continue in the absence of its founder, with no lessening of effectiveness, influence or reach.

It takes character and courage to entrust your hard work and successes into another's hand. Yet it has to be done if that work is going to outlive you. The wisdom behind your willingness is that you get to fashion with your hands and personally breathe your life into the person or persons that will succeed you. Rather than wait until near the end of your life for people to fight over who gets what of your inheritance, you do well to think about who will succeed you early in your operation, as God did. The people you ought to delegate responsibility to (Day 44) should be the people that you want to feature in your plans for the expansion and continued growth of the work you started. Ideally your successors will be people who have watched you, learned from you, worked and walked alongside you. People to whom you have been a mentor and friend and with whom you have shared your vision. Such people, even though they may do things that you did not, to meet the challenges of the future, will want to be true to the principles that they grew up under. They will have seen the results of the manner of your life and will be keen to become disciples of your way.

you have seen you work become much more in your hands, be careful that you **do not allow your garden paradise, your wealthy place, your delightful land to be a threat from within.** (Day 48) The big picture you are involved in is bigger than you (day 54), which is why it cannot and must not be about you. There remains much to do but it should not be your hands doing it all, but the hands of your delegates; hands that you have trained. If your work is truly about the big picture, you must resist the temptation to possess and own it. You have to be willing to let go in order to pass the baton on to others. Your work has got to be able to continue without you. By without you, I am not just referring to the day you 'give up the ghost,' but to a situation whereby you are no longer hands on with the project you initiated. Now you stand in a different relationship to it, watch from a distance and make yourself available to be consulted. You are no longer the main person — you have entrusted the work to another believing that they will be true to the values you taught them. If you have taught them well (Day 39), your work and influence will still be felt. It will not be any less without you, but more. If you have built well, your work will continue to speak after you have gone. It will be a mark that cannot be erased!

In your notebook, write down what would become of your life's work, your family, church, ministry, organisation, business, company, if you were no longer around? Have you made plans for your work to continue without you? If not, you need to plan and build with succession and expansion in mind!

Sustainability - Succession Planning

"A good leader does himself out of a job." Lao-Tzu

Day 56
Sabbath Week 8

Before I invite you to make your personal confessions of faith and to decide on this weeks' corresponding action, I want to summarise for you what we have discovered to date and how we might put them to work.

 Genesis 3 describes the approach of an enemy whose aim was to bring to an end the good things that Adam and Eve had going on in their environment. From what we know of this enemy he should have been resisted. (Day 50).

- Even though over 6 thousand years of God's dealings with humanity have come and gone, God continues to work His predetermined plan in the earth. He has not lessened in His passion to see the whole earth filled with the knowledge of the glory of God. He remains committed to the vision that was determined at the counsel of the Godhead in eternity past. (Day 51)

- At the end of the 6th day God assessed all that He had done and concluded that it was "very good" *(Genesis 1:31).* He was able to come to this summative judgment because His formative evaluations had given Him interim measures of the likely end result of all His activity. Because what God had determined at the planning phase of Creation had been achieved, there was no further need for Him to do any more. He had finished His work of creation and would be handing the rest of the work over to the person that He fashioned and breathed His life into (Day 55).

- In the Christian faith, the Judgement Seat of Christ is the place where each believer gets to hear God's summative evaluation of what they did with the life and the gifts He gave to them, before they enter His rest. (Day 52) The Judgement Seat of Christ will also be about rewards for service and will conclude with a time of rejoicing and celebration, a time where achievements are recognised, acknowledged and celebrated. (Day 53)

- The account of the Tower of Babel in Genesis 11 teaches that it is possible to achieve a measure of success by applying the *Principles of Creation* outlined in this book and still miss God's finest and best for your life. The account is a poignant reminder that our ideas will not succeed, ultimately, unless God is placed centrally. (Day 54)

 Not only must we be aware of the attitudes, habits and thoughts that if left unchecked or if we are ignorant about can cause us to self-sabotage, we must also do battle with threats from without— people whose aim is to bring to an end the work we are engaged in. These people are among the challenges that we have to see through if we are going to see the end of our faith and have reason to celebrate.

- To know ultimate success, our lives are life's work must place centrally the Kingdom of God. To receive the commendation, *"well 'run', good and faithful servant"* we have to run the race of our lives with all our might, stay faithful to our lane and pass what we have carried over *our* course to another, so that they might complete *their* own course.

I will not be ignorant; there are people in the world who do not want me to succeed. However, because I want to hear those all-important words, "well done good and faithful servant", I refuse to draw back and to be intimidated by those who dislike the big picture I have embraced.

Rather, I chose each day to maintain my walk of honesty and integrity, faithfulness and courage. I have committed myself to this work and I will not give in. By the grace of God, whose big picture has become my life and life's work, I will see every challenge through.

I am confident that at the end of my life I will hear the words "well done good and faithful servant". On the day of His return I expect to be a joy to my Creator. I give His will for my life my finest and best and will do what I can to raise up people who will continue to advance the big picture, until all families of the earth are blessed and His will is being done in the earth as it is being done in heaven.

 To take further the ideas of week 8, I will:

OLIVE VENTURE COACHING PLAN	
Stage 1: Desire Main Idea: The fire that burns within you	**Olive Theme** Day 1. *In His Image* Day 2. *It Starts When You …* Day 3. *Conceiving Ideas* Day 4. *The Seed of an Idea* Day 5. *A Burning Desire* Day 6. *Inside-Out*
Stage 2: Define Main Idea: What is this fire that burns within you?	Day 8. *What Do You Want?* Day 9. *Can You See It?* Day 10. *Can you Describe It ?* Day 11. *Why Do You Want it?*
Stage 3: Decide Main Idea: What will you do about the fire that burns within you?	Day 12. *How Comes After What & Why* Day 13. *A Definite Decision To Begin* Day 15. *Beginning* Day 16. *First Things First* Day 17. *Out Of Nothing* Day 18. *Beginning Again*
Stage 4: Design Main Idea: Make a plan for its full realisation	Day 19. *What Have You Got?* Day 20. *Utilising What You Have* Day 22. *Let Us* Day 23. *Whose Us?* Day 24. *Talking Answers* Day 25. *What Do You Think?* Day 26. *We Accord* Day 27. *I Accord* Day 29. *From Head to Hand* Day 30. *It is Written* Day 31. *Planning Your Work* Day 32. *SMART Goals*

Stage 5: Doing It	
Main Idea: Take deliberate and consistent actions towards making it real	Day 33. *The Power In Doing* Day 34. *Doing What You Do Best* Day 36. *Building By Design* Day 37. *Building On The Previous* Day 38. *Formative Evaluations* Day 39. *In Your Image* Day 40. *Put Life Into It* Day 41. *Working the Laws of Life* Day 43. *Speaking Well* Day 44. *Delegation And Partnership* Day 45. *Core Values and Core Business* Day 46. *Growth Potential* Day 47. *Multiple Streams Of Supply*
Stage 6: Difficulty Main Idea: Stay with it - persist, learn, change, grow	Day 48. *Threats From Within* Day 50. *Threats from Without* Day 51. *Seeing the Challenges Through*
Stage 7: Destiny Main Idea: Live the dream	Day 52. *Summative Evaluations* Day 53. *Celebrating Success* Day 54. *The Big Picture* Day 55. *Continuing Without You*

Abundance Mentality
A mindset that believes and reaches for more because so much more can be achieved without having to be greedy, competitive, jealous, possessive, or envious

Achievement with Virtue
The achievement of outward measures of success without compromising the qualities of good character like integrity, respect and honesty.

Action Planning
Thoughtful activity that precedes the implement of effective action.

Affirmations
Positive statements of faith that affirm one's beliefs, values and expectations.

Ambition
Strong desire for success and achievement of a specific goal.

Aspiration
Strong desire towards a definite goal.

Assertiveness
The external display of self confidence.

Attitude of Gratitude
A generally appreciative and valuing attitude towards life.

Brainstorming
The unrestrained airing of initial thoughts for external analysis.

Coaching
The process of working with the motivation of another towards achievement of a goal.

Cognitive Dissonance
An uneasy and unclear state of mind caused by conflicting information/feelings.

Collaboration
Working harmoniously with others towards achievement of a shared goal.

Congruence
Intra-personal agreement between thoughts, feelings and behaviour.

Corresponding Activity
Relevant actions that lead towards the achievement of specific aim.

Covenant
Unequivocal commitment and loyalty between two or more people for each other because of their shared purpose & core values.

Desire
A strong inclination towards some thing.

Dream Thieves
Threats from within and without that hinder dreams from being realised.

Enthusiasm
Energy and desire for a cause or purpose that is not easily quelled.

Faith
Actions that confirm that you know what you believe can be achieved.

Failure
An opportunity to learn from what has not gone according to plan.

Fear
The debilitating feeling caused by negative imagining that frustrates faith.

First Birth Potential
The abilities human beings possess because they are created in the image of God.

Five WH Planning Approach
The who, what, when, where, why and how approach to planning SMART.

Frustration
The feelings of agitation when passion and potential are blocked or incommensurably expressed.

Goal Clarification
The process of coming to a definite goal that is consistent with one's values, passions and beliefs.

Group Dynamics
The conscious and subconscious factors, processes and interactions between people in group situations.

Human Givens Christian Education
A biblical paradigm that advocates the full use of the resources of our first and second birth to design, develop and deliver a God honouring, eternally significant work in the earth.

Imagination
The release of the mind to conceive and create mental images of things not yet seen or experienced.

Individual Genius
The unique abilities, resources and powers in each person to make their life work.

Initiative
Being motivated from within to make a start, to have a go, to make the first move, to take action.

Kingdom of God
The authoritative and pervasive influence of God in and over the earth.

Kingdom Priorities
Giving precedence and primary place to things that pertain to the Kingdom of God.

Lateral Thinking
Imaginative, unconventional thinking that draws on latent sources of knowledge.

Law of Accumulation
The notion that our present life experience is the sum total of what we have gathered and used.

Law of Cause and Effect
The belief that everything in our universe, including our present life experience, have been caused.

Law of Expression
The notion that our present life experience is an outward manifestation of our dominant thoughts and feelings.

Law of Inertia
The notion that we lose what we do not make good and frequent use of.

Learning from the Past
The incredible opportunity to use every experience to our advantage.

Learning Intelligence
The unique ways in which each person learns best.

Legitimate Authority
The right and privilege to act and speak on another's behalf.

Leverage
Actions and attitudes that give us a favourable and advantageous starting point.

Locus of Control
The place where control, power and influence resides, according to the perception of an individual, for example, in their own hands/in the hands of some other.

Logos
The written word, in non- theological terms, an authoritative written document which contains information about things requiring action.

Meditation
To think about, consider, muse over, ponder and talk through with self.

Mentoring
The process of helping another to become more able at doing some thing.

Mind Mapping
A lateral and visual approach to representing ideas, thoughts and information in ways that support the human brain.

Mission Statement
A written statement that sets out our goals and the purpose behind our activity.

Motive Clarification
The process of becoming clear about our reasons for wanting.

Multiple Intelligence
The various ways in which people can be said to be intelligent.

Nature/Nurture Experience
The internal and external factors that contribute to a person's unique life experience.

Parallel Planning
A planning approach that has a viable alternative running alongside our chosen course of action.

Partnership
Working with each other for mutual benefit and increased productivity.

Passion
What an individual feels most affectionate about, internal stirrings that prompt action.

Perception
Our inner image/personal view of the world.

Personal Empowerment
Actions and attitudes, thoughts, values and beliefs that encourage and support an individual in taking effective action.

Personal Development
A process of realising personal potential in order to become ever increasingly what God imagined for you in all areas of your life.

Personal Inventory
Comprehensive knowledge of all that you have going for you.

Personal Power
Your ability to take action, to affect things, to influence and make things happen.

Personal Responsibility
Taking charge of yourself because you accept that the locus of control resides in and with you.

Possibility Thinking
A mindset/general attitude to life that gives faith impetus; the mindset that perceives opportunity in every difficult situation.

Problem Solving
A specific decision making approach that focuses on overcoming and making the best use of difficult situations.

Procrastination
To put off/delay taking necessary action.

Project Management
The skills of effectively managing a discrete piece of work from design to delivery.

Reality Checking
Having regard for how things really are, the realities of a situation.

Re-Languaging
Changing our vocabulary so that the words we speak support us in taking effective action.

Resolve
Following through on the promise you made to yourself to never give up.

Rhema
In non- theological terms, a word that requires you to take immediate action, a timely word for the present, a word in season.

Risk Management
Identifying and managing the hazards, threats, dangers within a given situation/decision.

Sabbath Principle
Taking time out to review activity, to refresh oneself, to restore one's energies for the next venture.

Second Birth Potential
The additional resources we have available to us by virtue of our being in Christ, for example peace with God, righteousness, the Holy Spirit.

Self-Awareness
To possess knowledge and understanding of the working of yourself.

Self Concept
The general view that you have of yourself.

Self Confidence
Having an assured, poised, secure view of your whole self.

Self Efficacy Beliefs
Belief in your ability to take effective action, to achieve your desires and goals.

Self-Esteem
A healthy regard for yourself based on your self concept and your self efficacy beliefs

Self Expression
The outward release of your thoughts, feelings and desires

Self Sabotage
Self-generated attitudes, thoughts and behaviours that undermine what you have achieved or want to achieve

Skills Inventory
Comprehensive knowledge of the things that you can do; your abilities and talents

Skills Mix
The range and blend of abilities, resources, talents and expertise within a group

Strategy
A practical and thoroughly planned approach to carrying out decisive action

Strategy Document
The document that outlines the details of your strategy

Success Criteria
The measures against which you judge the effectiveness and outcome of your actions

Succession Planning
Planning for the continuation and expansion of your work

Success Modelling
Learning from the walk and talk of people who have achieved with virtue what you want to accomplish

Sustainability
The inherent ability of your work to maintain itself

Synergy
The exponential dynamic that is present when individuals work with others to achieve their shared goals

Team Work
Individuals working together with others to achieve their shared goals

Thinking Skills
The use of a wide range of cognitive skills, logical and lateral thinking approaches to aid analysis, understanding, problem solving and decision making

Time Management
The effective use of your time

Vision
The mental picture you create and have in your mind of what you want to achieve

Visualisation
The use of the imagination to create mental pictures

Whole Brain Thinking
The use of lateral and logical thinking approaches to aid analysis, understanding, problem solving and decision making

Wisdom
The application of insightful and practical knowledge to a given situation

Olive Programmes

1. **Get Real - Biblical Perspectives on Life and Living** is a **Pastoral Care** resource that explores over 80 of the pressing concerns of life and living that people everywhere find challenging and frustrating. The Project conveys from a pastor-teacher perspective a biblical view of what goes on in our world and the principles that will enable us to live more completely and to handle these issues more effectively.

2. **Let there be Glory in the House of the Lord** is a **Church Health** resource that consists of over 40 topics that concern the administration of worship, fellowship, ministry and growth of the local church. The Project is delivered through an Olive Facilitator whose role is to stimulate the vision, motivation and involvement of people toward the development of their local church.

3. **Well Done Good and Faithful Servant** is a principle-centred, **Leadership Education** study. The purpose of the study is to stimulate our critical thinking around the foundational issues of leadership so that we might know how to be good and faithful stewards of the purpose and work we are engaged in. The Project is delivered through an Olive Tutor whose role is to work with leaders within a local church context.

4. **A More Excellent Way** is a comparative, **Christian Living** study that explores evidence supported, applied biblical values and principles of success and well being - contrasting them with habits and attitudes of ineffective living. The distinctions examined are considered essential for living and doing well in today's world and confirms that living life God's way is "A More Excellent Way."

5. **Distinctions** has been designed with two purposes in mind: **Evangelism** and **Christian Education.** In the first instance the Project uniquely outlines the Christian world view to non-believers so that they might understand its relevance for life and living. With regards to Christian Education, the Project helps believers develop a Christian mind set so that we think

theologically and practically about the issues of life and living and have a sound biblical philosophy for living effectively and in health in this world. For serious students of the Christian world view we offer the **Olive Branch Certificate in Applied Biblical Theology.**

6. **Principles of Creation** is a **Venture Education** study of the dynamic processes and principles involved in the biblical account of Creation and how these principles and processes can be practically and usefully applied to our life and life's work. The Programme is designed to help individuals and organisations to design and develop in their own image, a worthy enterprise, venture, quality of life and vision of their future.

7. **New Horizons** is an intensive, **Social Regeneration**, life skills education programme that coaches programme participants in the basic principles and practices of success and well-being achievement. The Programme is designed to help people from particularly disadvantaged communities develop the knowledge, motivation and confidence necessary to combat the social ills of poverty and social exclusion on a personal level.

8. **THRIVE, T**owards **H**ealth**, R**enewal, **I**ncreased **V**itality and **E**motionality, is an empowering, self help, **Health Education** programme that puts optimum physical, emotional and mental health into the hands of the individual. The programme helps individuals to better understand the workings of the human body and mind and to act on principles and practices of optimum health.

9. **Tips from the Top** is a principle – centred, **Personal Development** programme that draws on evidence supported knowledge of the art and science of success and well being. The Programme shows us how activating in new ways our ability to speak, think and decide, choose, take action and change, empowers us to handle the issues of our lives more effectively.

10. **Together We Can** explores over 40 issues of life and living and their implications for **Family Life and Parenting**- issues that people everywhere have found challenging and frustrating. The Project sensitively handles the issues through exercises, discussion, audio visuals, group work, problem solving case studies, art and crafts, games etc.

11. **Be Your Best - Youth Enrichment Curriculum** is a personal development/ life skills education programme that coaches youth between the ages of 13-19 in the basic principles and practices of success and well-being achievement. The Programme supports young people in designing ways to achieve their SMART educational, vocational and lifestyle goals and is premised on the belief that the potential of youth is realised and maximised through a supported process of learning and change.